Education Today 2013

THE OECD PERSPECTIVE

LB
14
.7
.E384
2012

D1715159

OECD

BETTER POLICIES FOR BETTER LIVES

This work is published on the responsibility of the Secretary-General of the OECD. The opinions expressed and arguments employed herein do not necessarily reflect the official views of the Organisation or of the governments of its member countries.

This document and any map included herein are without prejudice to the status of or sovereignty over any territory, to the delimitation of international frontiers and boundaries and to the name of any territory, city or area.

Please cite this publication as:
OECD (2012), *Education Today 2013: The OECD Perspective*, OECD Publishing.
http://dx.doi.org/10.1787/edu_today-2013-en

ISBN 978-92-64-17710-9 (print)
ISBN 978-92-64-18681-1 (PDF)

The statistical data for Israel are supplied by and under the responsibility of the relevant Israeli authorities. The use of such data by the OECD is without prejudice to the status of the Golan Heights, East Jerusalem and Israeli settlements in the West Bank under the terms of international law.

Photo credits:
Stocklib Image Bank © Cathy Yeulet
Stocklib Image Bank © Nailia Schwarz
Fotolia.com © Elenathewise
Fotolia.com © Franz Pfluegl
Fotolia.com © Kadal
Fotolia.com © pressmaster
Fotolia.com © rmarinello
Fotolia.com © Tan Kian Khoon

Corrigenda to OECD publications may be found on line at: *www.oecd.org/publishing/corrigenda*.

© OECD 2012

You can copy, download or print OECD content for your own use, and you can include excerpts from OECD publications, databases and multimedia products in your own documents, presentations, blogs, websites and teaching materials, provided that suitable acknowledgement of OECD as source and copyright owner is given. All requests for public or commercial use and translation rights should be submitted to *rights@oecd.org*. Requests for permission to photocopy portions of this material for public or commercial use shall be addressed directly to the Copyright Clearance Center (CCC) at *info@copyright.com* or the Centre français d'exploitation du droit de copie (CFC) at *contact@cfcopies.com*.

Foreword

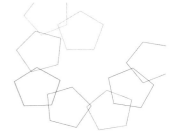

The OECD Directorate for Education helps member and non-member economies to foster human and social capital skills and leverage education and training systems to shape dynamic and sustainable futures. This means preparing learners for more rapid change than ever before. Key questions concern how skills can be matched to new needs, how to foster innovation, how to equip teachers for the 21st century, and how to reinforce the positive social impacts of education. We encourage countries to compare their performance and experience, and to learn from each other.

Education has been part of OECD work since the organisation was created 50 years ago but its importance over that time has grown markedly, both within countries' policy agendas and within the OECD itself. This growing prominence lay behind the decision to create a separate Directorate for Education in 2002. As reflected in this report's different chapters, we follow a "lifelong" approach to education and training. Our work also has a strong focus on quality, skills, equity, and innovation.

Knowledge management plays a key role in a world of information overload and knowledge-based economies. Traditionally, as OECD analyses have shown, education has not been exemplar in its own knowledge management, despite "knowledge" being education's core business. Given the significant volume of publications we produce each year, it is even more important that we provide a coherent overview of their key messages. This report aims to present the key findings and orientations for policy in an accessible way so that they can be used by different audiences – our own national contacts, other sections of governments, experts, media and the wider public – who do not have the time to stay abreast of all of the OECD's work on education. It is designed to encourage readers who know about only one or two of our studies to look further into those that they have been missing so far.

We have chosen to limit the scope of this report so that it includes only published results and policy orientations, and those applicable to most OECD countries (rather than, for example, single country reviews). The coverage is limited to work produced by the Directorate for Education, but it includes some analyses that have been conducted jointly with other OECD Directorates. A recent example is the OECD's horizontal "Skills Strategy" to which the Directorate for Education made an important contribution regarding education and innovation for skills.

Education Today: The OECD Perspective is only one example of the priority we have been giving recently to weaving the different strands of the Directorate's analyses more closely together and to highlighting our main messages, in addition to our longstanding annual flagship publication *Education at a Glance*. As part of the new GPS programme which we are

currently pursuing, we are establishing a knowledge management framework for our work on education, the integration of the evidence base from past and current analyses into this framework, and reinforcing the links between our education work programme and OECD's broader economic and social agenda. In 2009, we created an online collaborative space called *educationtoday* which offers relevant information, evidence and discussions on the impact of the crisis on education and related issues.

Following the positive response to the first edition of *Education Today: The OECD Perspective* published in March 2009, it was decided to make the report a regular feature and a second publication was released in October 2010. Within the Directorate for Education, this third synthesis has been undertaken by the Innovation and Measuring Progress Division with the text prepared by Marco Kools and David Istance, with the executive summary prepared by Sue Kendall (Public Affairs and Communications Directorate) and edited by Marilyn Achiron. Elisabeth Villoutreix and Elizabeth Del Bourgo were responsible for layout and proofreading, while Corinne Heckmann provided the statistical graphics and Amy Todd supported the data verification process. Cassandra Davis and Anne-Lise Prigent (Public Affairs and Communications Directorate) provided advice and co-ordination with the related dissemination activities within the Directorate.

The Directorate for Education is part of the OECD Secretariat and contributes to the Organisation's commitment to building a stronger, cleaner and fairer world economy.

We provide comparative data and analysis on education policy making to help build efficient and effective educational systems, and improve learning outcomes. We provide a forum where governments, business, civil society and academia can share best practices and learn from one another.

Our statistics and indicators provide a strong evidence base for international comparisons of all aspects of education systems. Our policy analyses facilitate peer learning across countries as new policy options are explored and experiences compared. Our future-oriented educational research helps shape policy agendas by identifying upcoming issues while drawing upon the overall breadth of the OECD's policy work.

Table of Contents

Table of Contents

Boxes

Figures

This book has...

StatLinkS
A service that delivers Excel® files from the printed page!

Look for the *StatLinks* at the bottom left-hand corner of the tables or graphs in this book.
To download the matching Excel® spreadsheet, just type the link into your Internet browser,
starting with the *http://dx.doi.org* prefix.
If you're reading the PDF e-book edition, and your PC is connected to the Internet, simply
click on the link. You'll find *StatLinks* appearing in more OECD books.

Note on Country Coverage and Levels of Education

Country coverage

OECD and partner countries: The different sources from different dates used in this volume mean that OECD membership may not be identical in all cases. The entries cover the 34 countries that were members of the OECD when this report was drafted, as well as a number of partner countries and territories.

The statistical data for Israel are supplied by and under the responsibility of the relevant Israeli authorities. The use of such data by the OECD is without prejudice to the status of the Golan Heights, East Jerusalem and Israeli settlements in the West Bank under the terms of international law.

Levels of education

Education systems vary considerably from country to country, including the ages at which students typically begin and end each phase of schooling, the duration of courses, and what is taught. To facilitate the compilation of internationally comparable statistics on education, the United Nations created an International Standard Classification of Education (ISCED), which provides a basis for comparing different education systems and a standard terminology.

Levels of education and ISCED classification

Pre-primary education/early childhood education ISCED 0
The first stage of organised education. Minimum entry age to pre-primary education is 3 years of age though "early childhood education and care" is not as restricted in terms of age or preparation for schooling.

Primary education ISCED 1
Designed to provide a sound basic education with entry age between 5 and 7 years of age. Duration tends to be 6 years.

Lower secondary education ISCED 2
Completes provision of basic education, usually with greater subject orientation. In some countries, the end of this level marks the end of compulsory education.

Upper secondary education ISCED 3
Even stronger subject specialisation than at lower secondary level, with teachers often more highly qualified. Students typically expected to have completed 9 years of education or lower secondary schooling before entry and are generally around the age of 15 or 16.

Post-secondary non-tertiary education ISCED 4
Programmes at this level may be regarded nationally as part of upper secondary or post-secondary education, but in terms of international comparison they are counted as post-secondary as entry typically requires completion of an upper secondary programme. Content may not be much more advanced than at upper secondary and is lower than at the tertiary level. Duration is usually equivalent to between 6 months and 2 years of full-time study.

Tertiary education ISCED 5 (sub-categories 5A and 5B)
ISCED 5 is the first stage of tertiary education. ISCED distinguishes between levels 5A (longer and more theoretical programmes) and 5B (programmes are shorter and more practically oriented). As tertiary education differs greatly between countries, the demarcation between these two sub-categories is not always clear cut.

Advanced research programmes ISCED 6
The second stage of tertiary education, devoted to advanced study and original research.

Readers should note that *Education Today 2013* may use simplified terminology from that used in the ISCED classification and in *Education at a Glance 2012*.

For fuller definitions and explanations of the ISCED classification:

ISCED 1997: *www.uis.unesco.org/Library/Documents/isced97-en.pdf*

ISCED 2011: *www.uis.unesco.org/Education/Documents/UNESCO_GC_36C-19_ISCED_EN.pdf*

Executive Summary

Countries need an increasingly educated and skilled workforce to succeed in today's knowledge economy. That means good basic education in childhood and adolescence that equips people not just for the jobs of today, but with the ability to learn new skills for the jobs of tomorrow right through their lifetime.

Education is for life, not for the classroom. Indeed, some of the most important skills for life and learning may be acquired before, after and outside school. The latest research shows that pupils who took part in pre-primary school programmes are more likely to have better educational outcomes at age 15. In the majority of OECD countries, most children benefit from pre-primary education before they are five, but it is important to ensure that it delivers quality care with equity of access, and that is a question of funding and organisation.

Increasing numbers of young people are completing secondary education, with girls overtaking boys, and tertiary education is also on the rise. For many countries the question now is not so much providing education, but ensuring its quality and equity of access regardless of gender and socio-economic status.

Teachers have a key role to play in delivering quality education, and feedback is increasingly important to help them cope with changing demands and curricula. The quality of programmes is driven by the need for foundation skills plus adaptability and ability to learn going forward; increasingly too education is not just a matter of national standards but ensuring quality in cross-border offerings.

And there is the crucial question of ensuring that education, whether secondary, vocational or tertiary, equips people with the skills actually needed in the workplace. Increasingly these are not just technical or job-specific skills, but "soft" skills such as the ability to adapt to change and the ability to learn.

With ageing populations and the need for people to retire later as life expectancy increases, we need to know if older people can adapt and keep learning. Brain research says yes, but only 1.5% of over-40s are enrolled in formal education, compared with 6% of 30-39 year-olds. We can no longer afford this reluctance: a cultural shift is needed by policy makers, employers and the employees themselves to make best use of their talents. If someone starts work at age 22 and is going to work up to an official retirement age of 66, for example, they will still have a quarter of their working life ahead of them at 55. A lot of change can happen in those 11 years, so people will need to stay ready to learn, and employers will need to be ready to retrain them.

POLICY DIRECTIONS

Early Childhood Education and Care
- Place well-being, early development and learning at the core of early childhood approaches
- Provide autonomy, funding and support to early childhood services, linked to delivery of quality services
- Improve staff qualifications, training and working conditions
- Engage families and communities

Schooling: Investments, Organisation and Learners
- Develop skills for effective school leadership and make it an attractive profession
- Increase job differentiation between new and experienced teachers to improve effectiveness
- Promote greater computer use at school and experimental research on its effects

Transition Beyond Initial Education
- Ensure that vocational education provides the right mix of skills for the labour market
- Reform career guidance to develop well-informed career advice for all
- Make full use of workplace learning

Higher Education
- Develop a vision for tertiary education and sound instruments for implementing that vision
- Use cost-sharing between state and students as the principle for tertiary education funding
- Improve cost-effectiveness
- Improve the quality of teaching

Lifelong Learning and Adults
- Develop system-level policies for effective adult learning
- Ensure successful co-financing of adult learning
- Promote active debate on the nature of teaching, learning and assessment
- Devote the necessary resources of people, time and money

Outcomes, Benefits and Returns
- Foster student interest in science, mathematics and technology
- Aim to secure similar student performance among schools
- Clarify returns to training by augmenting information and removing structural barriers
- Parental engagement in a child's education needs to be continuous and start at birth

Equity and Equality of Opportunity

- Eliminate grade repetition
- Manage school choice to avoid segregation and increased inequities
- Reinforce learning the host language for immigrant children
- Target low performance regardless of background

Innovation and Knowledge Management

- Equip people with skills for innovation
- Enable women to play a larger role in the innovation process
- Make better links between educational research, policy and practice

Introduction

This summary report is based on results from OECD work produced in recent years by the Directorate for Education, and especially in the past three to four years. The background to its preparation is explained in the Foreword. The approach chosen focuses on results and policy orientations which are published and hence in the public domain. Only generalised findings about developments, policy or practice relevant across most OECD countries have been included. So, not covered are: studies or reviews of single countries; publications which provide exchange of information on promising practice without broader analytical conclusions; work plans and programme intentions; and clarifying statements of problems, challenges or issues.

As with the 2010 edition of *Education Today*, the publication is divided into eight chapters, devised as a structure to reflect well the different areas of educational work and to bring out policy conclusions and messages. It is produced entirely in modular format rather than as a continuous narrative. Each of the sections is divided into, respectively, *Introduction, Key Findings* and *Policy Directions*. Each modular text is introduced by the key message it contains or, where the module is in the form of a list of messages, these are highlighted instead. Each text also includes the title and chapter reference to the OECD report from which it comes, and these titles are brought together in a bibliography at the end of each chapter. A selection of illustrative figures and boxes has also been included to complement the text. This report uses the OECD *StatLinks* service and below each table and figure is a stable URL.

In reporting findings and conclusions, the volume avoids reference to specific projects, organisational units and internal structures within the Directorate for Education as these are largely uninteresting to the external audience. The introductions to each chapter do, however, make some connection to particular projects and future plans as an additional signpost for linking outcomes and messages to the work being undertaken.

In order to stay within manageable limits, this resource is highly selective of all the possible findings and policy orientations regarding education at the OECD. As the included texts are removed from the fuller analyses from which they are taken, there is a natural risk of over-simplification with short conclusions taken out of their wider analytical context. For both of these reasons, therefore, it is strongly advised that users looking for more than the headline messages should refer back to the original OECD source for the fuller picture.

1

Early Childhood Education and Care

Participation in education by three- and four-year-olds tends now to be high, though coverage is a third or less of the age group in several OECD countries. Early childhood education and care (ECEC) has been a growing priority in OECD countries, and the subject of past and ongoing OECD analysis. A major OECD review was published in 2006 – Starting Strong II: Early Childhood Education and Care *– which has been followed up through an ongoing international network. There are wide differences between systems, including between those which have a strong "preparation for school" approach and those implementing a broader social pedagogy, between those with mainly public provision and those relying strongly on private household resources, as well as in the relative emphasis on education and childcare. ECEC can bring a wide range of benefits for children, parents and society at large, but the magnitude of benefits is conditional on quality. Therefore the OECD in 2012 released* Starting Strong III: A Quality Toolbox for Early Childhood Education and Care, *which serves as a reference guide and aims to encourage quality in ECEC. Additionally, the 2012 edition of* Education at a Glance: OECD Indicators *includes a new indicator on the state of early childhood education, providing a rich comparative insight into early childhood education systems around the world.*

The statistical data for Israel are supplied by and under the responsibility of the relevant Israeli authorities. The use of such data by the OECD is without prejudice to the status of the Golan Heights, East Jerusalem and Israeli settlements in the West Bank under the terms of international law.

INTRODUCTION

Early childhood provision – pre-primary and childcare – has been a growing priority in many countries. Such priority is manifest by many parents, who tend more and more to be both employed while their children are young. It is also a phase of education and services increasingly recognised as important in its contribution to a wide range of social, economic and educational goals. At the same time, it is a sector with a complex diversity of players and partners, and one with a significant lack of investment in many countries.

A major OECD review in the field of early childhood – *Starting Strong II: Early Childhood Education and Care,* published in 2006 – was a follow-up to an earlier international review published in 2001. Its policy orientations are broadly focused on overcoming the under-developed status of the sector that remains typical of many countries. In recognition that early interventions are conditional on their quality, the OECD published the third in the *Starting Strong* series in 2012 - *Starting Strong III: A Quality Toolbox for Early Childhood Education and Care* - which defines "quality" and serves as a reference guide for those involved in shaping early childhood education and care. The Starting Strong Network has continued to help countries to develop effective and efficient approaches, and good practice in the field of early childhood education and care (ECEC). It does so through its clearing house of new policy research, data and methodology development, workshops, and by fostering contacts among professionals worldwide.

The 2012 edition of *Education at a Glance* includes a new indicator on the state of early childhood education, and as such provides a rich comparative insight into the early childhood education systems around the world. Future policy work will continue to investigate how policies can promote and enhance quality, and how they can effectively be put in place. It will focus on monitoring the quality in ECEC and the development of internationally comparable indicators.

KEY FINDINGS

In the majority of countries – but not all – education now begins for most well before the age of 5: Already over three-quarters of 4-year-olds (79%) are enrolled in early childhood education programmes across OECD countries, and this rises to 83% in the OECD countries that are part of the European Union. Enrolment rates for early childhood education at this age vary from over 95% in Belgium, France, Germany, Iceland, Italy, Japan, Luxembourg, Mexico, the Netherlands, New Zealand, Norway, Spain and the United Kingdom, at one end of the spectrum, to less than 60% in Australia, Canada, Finland, Greece, Poland, Switzerland and Turkey. The highest enrolments of 3-year-olds in early childhood education are found in Belgium, France, Iceland, Italy, Norway and Spain with rates of more than 90%.

📖 *Education at a Glance 2012: OECD Indicators,* 2012, Indicator C2

Demand for early childhood provision for those aged under 3 years far outstrips supply in many countries: Though in some OECD countries the majority of the children under 3 years are in early childhood education and care, in most the supply of these services falls well short of meeting demands. The highest enrolments of 3-year-olds in early childhood programmes are found in Belgium (99%), France (100%), Iceland (95%), Italy (93%), Norway (95%) and Spain (99%). On the other side of the spectrum are Australia, Canada, and Switzerland both with 10% or less of 3-year-olds in early childhood programmes. OECD research has found that the demand for services for these young children is significantly higher than the places available in many countries, even in those with provisions for long parental leave. In countries where public funding for parental leave is limited, many working parents must either seek solutions in the private market, where ability to pay significantly influences accessibility to quality services, or else rely on informal arrangements with family, friends and neighbours.

📖 *Education at a Glance 2012: OECD Indicators*, 2012, Indicator C2; *Starting Strong III: A Quality Toolbox for Early Childhood Education and Care*, 2012

Figure 1.1.

Enrolment rates at age four in early childhood and primary education (2005 and 2010)

Full-time and part-time pupils in public and private institutions

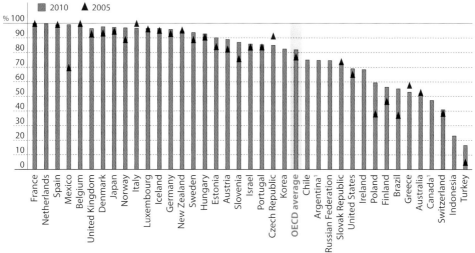

1. Year of reference 2009.

Countries are ranked in descending order of the enrolment rates of 4-year-olds in 2010.

Source: OECD (2012), *Education at a Glance 2012: OECD Indicators*, OECD Publishing. Argentina and Indonesia: UNESCO Institute for Statistics (World Education Indicators programme). Table C2.1. See Annex 3 for notes (*www.oecd.org/edu/eag2012*).

StatLink 🔗📊 http://dx.doi.org/10.1787/888932663055

Publicly-funded pre-primary provision tends to be more strongly developed in the European than in the non-European countries of the OECD: In Europe, the concept of universal access of 3-6 year-olds is generally accepted. Most countries in this region provide all children with at least two years of free, public-funded provision before they begin primary provision. With the exception of Ireland and the Netherlands, such access is a statutory

right from the age of 3 years and in some even before. Early education programmes in Europe tend to be free and often located in schools. In OECD countries outside Europe, free early education tends to be only available from age 5, though many children are enrolled from age 4 in Australia, Korea and some US states. On average in OECD countries 18% of expenditure of pre-primary institutions comes from private sources. However, this proportion varies widely: ranging from 5% or less in Belgium, Estonia, Luxembourg, the Netherlands and Sweden, at one end of the spectrum, to over 48% in Australia, Japan and Korea, at the other.

📖 *Starting Strong II: Early Childhood Education and Care,* 2006, Chapter 4; *Education at a Glance 2012: OECD Indicators,* 2012, Indicator C2

Figure 1.2.
Expenditure on early childhood education institutions as a percentage of GDP (2009)
By funding source

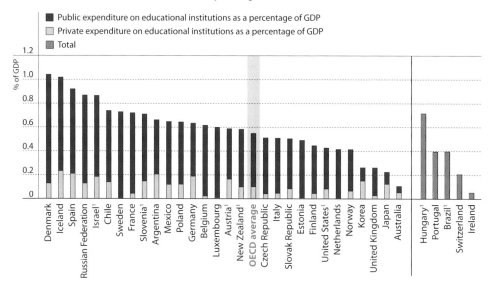

1. Includes some expenditure on childcare.
Countries are ranked in descending order of public and private expenditure on educational institutions.
Source: OECD (2012), *Education at a Glance 2012: OECD Indicators,* OECD Publishing. Argentina: UNESCO Institute for Statistics (World Education Indicators programme). Table C2.2. See Annex 3 for notes (*www.oecd.org/edu/eag2012*).

StatLink ᵐˢᴾ http://dx.doi.org/10.1787/888932663074

Participation in pre-primary programmes tends to lead to better later outcomes: PISA results (2009) show that in all OECD countries 15-year-old students who attended pre-primary education for more than one year on average outperformed students who did not. This finding stands, even after socio-economic background is accounted for. The difference between students who have attended pre-primary for more than one year and those who have not attended pre-primary at all averaged 54 score points in the PISA reading assessment – or more than one year of formal schooling. PISA research also shows that students perform better when they have been enrolled in pre-primary programmes of longer duration, with lower child-to-teacher ratios and higher expenditures per child.

📖 *Education at a Glance 2012: OECD Indicators,* 2012, Indicator C2; *PISA 2009 Results: Overcoming Social Background: Equity in Learning Opportunities and Outcomes,* 2010, Chapter 5

There are 14 children for each staff member at the pre-primary level in OECD countries, with wide variations: Child-to-staff ratios play a key role in ensuring quality for better child development. The ratio of children to teaching staff is also an important indicator of the resources devoted to education. On average in OECD countries, there are 14 children for every teacher. The child-to-teacher ratio ranges from more than 20 in France, Israel, Mexico, Turkey and the partner country China, to fewer than 10 in Chile, Estonia, Iceland, New Zealand, Slovenia and Sweden. Some countries, e.g. Ireland and Israel, make extensive use of teachers' aides at the pre-primary level.

📖 *Starting Strong II: Early Childhood Education and Care,* 2006; *Education at a Glance 2012: OECD Indicators,* 2012, Indicator C2

Figure 1.3.
Ratio of children to teaching staff in early childhood education (2010)
Public and private institutions

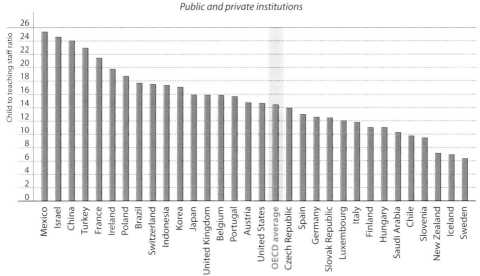

Countries are ranked in descending order of children to teaching staff ratios in early childhood education.
Source: OECD (2012), *Education at a Glance 2012: OECD Indicators,* OECD Publishing. China and Indonesia: UNESCO Institute for Statistics (World Education Indicators programme). Saudi Arabia: UNESCO Institute for Statistics. Table C2.2. See Annex 3 for notes (www.oecd.org/edu/eag2012).

StatLink ᵐᵖ🔗 http://dx.doi.org/10.1787/888932663093

Two broad emphases in early education characterise different countries – preparing for school and social pedagogy: OECD countries approach the partnership between early childhood services and primary school in different ways – all trying to improve the co-ordination between the sectors but starting from different premises. Broadly, there are two different approaches across countries. France and the English-speaking countries tend to see the question of partnership from the point of view of the school: early education should serve the objectives of public education and provide children with "readiness for school" skills. In contrast, countries inheriting the social pedagogy tradition (the Nordic and Central European countries) see this sector more to support families and the broad development needs of young children.

📖 *Starting Strong II: Early Childhood Education and Care,* 2006, Chapter 3

A positive consequence of decentralisation has been the integration of early childhood education and care services at the local level, leading to a more efficient allocation of resources to children: New services tend to be less bound by traditional competency boundaries than government departments. Many local authorities in Austria, Denmark, Finland, France, Hungary, Germany, Italy, the Netherlands, Norway, Sweden, the United Kingdom and the United States have brought together children's services and education portfolios to plan more effectively and provide coherence of services for young children and their families. Some local authorities have integrated administration and policy development across age groups and sectors. In Denmark, Italy, Norway, Sweden and the United Kingdom, for example, an increasing number of local authorities have reorganised responsibility for early childhood education and care, and for schools (and sometimes other children's services) under one administrative department and political committee.

📖 *Starting Strong II: Early Childhood Education and Care,* 2006, Chapter 2

POLICY DIRECTIONS

Early childhood education and care policy needs to be systemic and integrate the different forms of early childhood provision, allow universal access, and enjoy a strong and equal partnership with the rest of the education system. The *Starting Strong II* review of this sector proposes ten policy areas for consideration:

- **Place well-being, early development and learning at the core of early childhood approaches:** Rather than being an adjunct to labour market policies with weak development agendas or an underresourced "Cinderella" education service, early childhood education and care needs to have the child and her/his well-being and learning at the core.

- **Aspire towards early childhood education and care systems that support broad learning, participation and democracy:** The touchstones of a democratic approach are to extend the agency of the child and right of parents to be involved in the education of their children. Learning to be, learning to do, learning to learn, and learning to live together are the critical elements to be promoted in each child.

- **Provide autonomy, funding and support to early childhood services:** Within the parameters of system-wide goals and guidelines, educators and services should have the autonomy to plan and to choose curricula for the children in their care; policy should provide the means for staff to exercise such autonomy and participatory approaches.

- **Develop with the stakeholders broad guidelines and curricular standards for all early childhood education and care services:** Guiding frameworks – especially when they have been developed together by the key stakeholders – help to promote a more even quality across early childhood provision, to guide and support professional staff, and to facilitate communication between staff and families.

- **Base public funding on achieving quality pedagogical goals:** Most countries need to double their annual investment per child to ensure child-staff ratios and qualified staff on some parity with the primary sector; the investment should be directed to achieving quality pedagogical goals rather than simply aiming to create sufficient places.

- **Improve the working conditions and professional education of early childhood education and care staff:** The OECD reviews found a number of common weaknesses that need attention. These are: low recruitment and pay levels, particularly in childcare services; lack of certification in specialist early childhood pedagogy; excessive feminisation of staff; and lack of diversity of staff to reflect neighbourhood diversity.

- **Create the governance structures necessary for system accountability and quality assurance:** These include such elements as strong expert policy units, data collection and monitoring capacity, an evaluation agency, and a pedagogical advisory or inspection corps.

- **Attend to the social context of early childhood development:** Well-organised services should work towards a broad but realistic vision to which the other stakeholders can subscribe, serving at the same time to support parents in child-rearing, facilitate women working, and help social inclusion for low income and immigrant families.

- **Encourage family and community involvement in early childhood services:** The continuity of children's experience across the different early childhood education and care environments is greatly enhanced when parents and staff members share information and adopt consistent approaches to socialisation, daily routines, child development and learning; communities are important both as providers and as offering space for partnerships.

- **Reduce child poverty and exclusion through fiscal, social and labour policies, and increase resources for children with additional learning rights within universal programmes:** Research indicates the effectiveness of universal programmes for children with different disabilities and disadvantages, combined with enhanced funding and investment in quality services, rather than targeted programmes which serve to segregate and stigmatise.

📖 *Starting Strong II: Early Childhood Education and Care,* 2006, Chapter 10

Research emphasises that realising the benefits depends on the quality of the early interventions. The OECD "toolbox" on the quality of early childhood education and care (ECEC) presents five "policy levers" for action:

- **Setting out quality goals and regulations:** Setting out explicit quality goals and regulations can help align resources with prioritised areas, promote more co-ordinated child-centred services, level the playing field for providers, and help parents make informed choices.

- **Designing and implementing curriculum standards:** Curriculum or learning standards can promote more even quality for ECEC provision across different settings, help staff to enhance pedagogical strategies, and help parents to better understand child development.

- **Improving qualifications, training and working conditions:** ECEC staff play the key role in ensuring healthy child development and learning; areas for reform include qualifications, initial education, professional development and working conditions.

- **Engaging families and communities:** Parents and communities should be regarded as partners working towards the same goal. Home learning environments and neighbourhood matter for healthy child development and learning.

- **Advancing data collection, research and monitoring:** Data, research and monitoring are powerful tools for improving children's outcomes and driving continuous improvement in service delivery.

📖 *Starting Strong III: A Quality Toolbox for Early Childhood Education and Care,* 2012, Executive Summary

References and Further Reading

OECD (2006), *Starting Strong II: Early Childhood Education and Care*, OECD Publishing.

OECD (2008), *Students with Disabilities, Learning Difficulties and Disadvantages: Policies, Statistics and Indicators*, OECD Publishing.

OECD (2010), *PISA 2009 Results: Overcoming Social Background: Equity in Learning Opportunities and Outcomes (Volume II)*, PISA, OECD Publishing.

OECD (2012), *Starting Strong III: A Quality Toolbox for Early Childhood Education and Care*, OECD Publishing.

OECD (2012), *Education at a Glance 2012: OECD Indicators*, OECD Publishing.

2

Schooling: Investments, Organisation and Learners

There have been major investments in schooling across OECD countries, including in teacher salaries. Shared patterns exist alongside notable differences such as in teacher beliefs (as charted with the Teaching and Learning International Survey [TALIS]) and in school time use. OECD work has analysed the characteristics of learners and learning, teachers, and how to improve school leadership. The analytical work undertaken for the annual International Summit on the Teaching Profession recognises the key role of teachers for the success of schooling and educational change. PISA studies have permitted specific analyses of aspects of schooling, such as student attitudes towards and knowledge of the environment. Work on the educational role of technology has shown how important is home use for educational outcomes. Policy orientations on schooling have stressed the need to professionalise and innovate, calling for reforms directed at effective learning to be placed at the core of schooling, rather than changing only structures and administrative systems. The OECD continues to analyse and stress the value of good school design and safe buildings.

The statistical data for Israel are supplied by and under the responsibility of the relevant Israeli authorities. The use of such data by the OECD is without prejudice to the status of the Golan Heights, East Jerusalem and Israeli settlements in the West Bank under the terms of international law.

INTRODUCTION

The period of compulsory education – primary, lower secondary and even the upper secondary cycle in some countries – is at the core of all education systems. Over recent years, there have been significant investments in this core phase of education, recognised as fundamental for laying the foundation on which so many other social, economic and educational outcomes may follow. OECD work has therefore analysed with growing precision the characteristics of learners, teachers and the nature of school practices, including leadership.

Teachers (and the educational workforce in general) are widely recognised as central to the success of schooling and their role in educational change; a position that is endorsed by the work of the OECD and in recent years most prominently through the analytical work undertaken in support of the annual "International Summit on the Teaching Profession" (i.e. OECD 2011 and OECD 2012). *Improving School Leadership* has provided in-depth analyses of different approaches to school leadership as well as practical guidelines for improvement.

The Teaching and Learning International Survey (TALIS) in 2008 was based on the experience of some 90 000 lower secondary teachers and school principals in 23 countries; first results were published in 2009. The second cycle of TALIS will be conducted in 2013 in which countries will have the option to expand the survey to primary and upper secondary schools. The OECD triennial Programme for International Student Assessment (PISA) surveys, in 2009 conducted in 65 countries and economies worldwide, rising to 72 in 2012, have permitted focused analyses of schooling, ranging from the attitudes and awareness of students, through features of the learning environment, to the allocation of resources. The work of the Centre for Educational Research and Innovation (CERI) on, for instance, learning environments and on the use of technology in education has offered a complementary set of international studies on aspects of schooling. The Centre for Effective Learning Environments (CELE) has continued to identify how best to design and deliver safe, healthy and high-quality educational facilities.

KEY FINDINGS

Only a small minority of students in OECD and partner countries do not complete compulsory education: Participation in education tends to be high in most OECD countries and partner countries until the end of compulsory education, with more than 90% completing this phase in most. Those where more that 10% do not complete the end of compulsory education are: Australia, Belgium, Chile, Germany, Hungary, Israel, Mexico, the Netherlands, Turkey and the United States, and among the partner countries with data available Argentina, Brazil, Indonesia and the Russian Federation. The age which marks the end of compulsory attendance, however, is relatively late in 10 of these 14 OECD countries and partner countries at 17 or 18 years of age [the exceptions being Mexico (15 years of age) and Turkey (14 years of age), for the partner country Indonesia (15 years of age)].

📖 *Education at a Glance 2012: OECD Indicators*, 2012, Indicator C1

Spending per student in schooling (plus post-secondary non-tertiary) has increased everywhere in OECD countries since 2000, contrasting with a mixed picture in tertiary education: Using 100 as the index for spending per school student in 2005, this indicator of change had risen to 115 by 2009 in OECD countries, well up from the OECD average 74 in 2000. (This compares with 109 for spending per tertiary education student in 2009 compared with 2005 levels, with the index falling over this time in several countries.) Even in only the short period since 2005, the rise in spending per school student was very marked in some countries, with the index reaching 148 in the Slovak Republic and among parter countries, 166 in Brazil and 158 in the Russian Federation.

📖 *Education at a Glance 2012: OECD Indicators,* 2012, Indicator B1

Figure 2.1.

Relative expenditure per student by educational institutions for all services at different levels of education (2009)

Primary education = 100

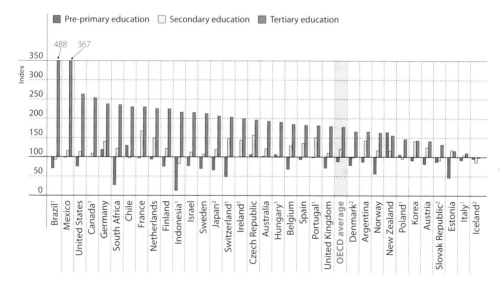

Notes: A ratio of 300 for tertiary education means that expenditure per tertiary student by educational institutions is three times the expenditure per primary student by educational institutions.

A ratio of 50 for pre-primary education means that exenditure per pre-primary pupil by educational institutions is half the expenditure per primary student by educational institutions.

1. Public institutions only.

2. Some levels of education are included with others. Refer to "x" code in Table B1.1a for details.

Countries are ranked in descending order of expenditure per student by educational institutions in tertiary education relative to primary education.

Source: OECD (2012), *Education at a Glance 2012: OECD Indicators,* OECD Publishing. Argentina, Indonesia: UNESCO Institute for Statistics (World Education Indicators programme). South Africa: UNESCO Institute for Statistics. Table B1.1a. See Annex 3 for notes (www.oecd.org/edu/eag2012).

StatLink ᝀᓵ http://dx.doi.org/10.1787/888932662485

Expenditure by educational institutions on each student rises with the level of education in almost all OECD countries: The expenditure per student at the secondary level is on average 1.2 times greater than at the primary level. This ratio exceeds 1.5 in the Czech Republic, France and Portugal. Educational institutions in OECD countries spend, on average, 1.8 times more per tertiary student than for each primary pupil, but patterns vary widely. For example, Austria, Estonia, Iceland, Italy, Korea, Poland and the Slovak Republic spend less than 1.5 times on a tertiary student than on a primary pupil, while Mexico spends three times as much or even more.

📖 *Education at a Glance 2012: OECD Indicators,* 2012, Indicator B1

In most systems, there are more students in lower secondary classes than in primary classes: At the lower secondary level the average class in OECD countries has more than 23 students compared to 21 students at the primary level. In Greece, Japan, Korea, Mexico and Poland, the average class has four more or greater students in lower secondary schools compared with primary schools. The exceptions to the general pattern are the United Kingdom and, to a lesser extent, Switzerland. Class sizes vary considerably among countries. For example, at the lower secondary level, class sizes of 20 or fewer in Denmark, Estonia, Finland, Iceland, Luxembourg, Slovenia, Switzerland (public institutions) and the United Kingdom, and partner country the Russian Federation, compared with more than 34 per class in Korea, and over 50 in partner country China.

📖 *Education at a Glance 2012: OECD Indicators,* 2012, Indicator D2

Figure 2.2.
Average class size in primary and secondary education (2010)

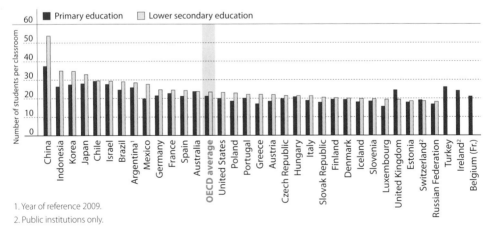

1. Year of reference 2009.
2. Public institutions only.
Countries are ranked in descending order of average class size in lower secondary education.
Source: OECD (2012), *Education at a Glance 2012: OECD Indicators,* OECD Publishing. Argentina, China, Indonesia: UNESCO Institute for Statistics (World Education Indicators programme). Table D2.1. See Annex 3 for notes (*www.oecd.org/edu/eag2012*).

StatLink ㎳ http://dx.doi.org/10.1787/888932663625

In most OECD countries teachers' salaries in primary and secondary education increased in real terms between 2000 and 2010: Between 2000 and 2010, teachers' salaries in primary, lower secondary and upper secondary increased in real terms in most OECD countries. In Denmark, Estonia, Ireland, Portugal and Scotland salaries increased at all three levels of education by at least 20%. In the Czech Republic (primary and lower secondary levels) and in Turkey salaries doubled over the past decade. Only in France and Japan among those with data did teachers' salaries decrease in real terms by more than 5%. Mostly, salaries increased less since 2005. The exceptions to this pattern are Denmark, Estonia, Israel (primary and lower secondary levels), the Netherlands (lower secondary level) and New Zealand, where most of the increase in teachers' salaries occurred after 2005.

📖 *Education at a Glance 2012: OECD Indicators,* 2012, Indicator D3

Some countries use a "career-based" model of teacher employment and others a "position-based" model, each with its own strengths and weaknesses: In "career-based" systems, teachers expect to stay long in the public service after early entry and once recruited are allocated to posts according to internal rules (e.g. France, Japan, Korea and Spain). These systems tend to avoid problems of teacher shortages but with concerns about how far teacher education is connected to school and student needs, and with lack of incentives for continued professional development and of responsiveness to local needs. "Position-based" systems instead tend to select the "best" candidate for each position, whether by external recruitment or internal promotion, with wider access to the profession in terms of age or previous career experience (e.g. Canada, Sweden, Switzerland and the United Kingdom). The problems typically encountered in these systems are teacher shortages, especially in mathematics, sciences, etc., difficulties in ensuring a core of good older teachers, and wider teacher quality gaps between attractive and unattractive districts/schools.

📖 *Teachers Matter: Attracting, Developing and Retaining Effective Teachers,* 2005, Executive Summary

Substantial differences exist between countries in teacher beliefs about how teaching should be delivered: In most countries teachers see their job as helping students actively to develop and construct their knowledge rather than concentrate on transmitting content only (among the TALIS countries, the exception is Italy where only a minority endorses this view). A clear majority of teachers support a constructivist approach in Australia, Korea, North-Western Europe and Scandinavia, whereas belief in direct transmission is much more in evidence in Malaysia, South America and Southern Europe. Teachers in Eastern Europe lie in between in the balance of teachers having mainly constructivist or mainly transmission beliefs.

📖 *Creating Effective Teaching and Learning Environments: First Results from TALIS,* 2009, Chapter 4 and Executive Summary

TALIS data permit analysis of the teaching practices and teachers' participation in professional learning communities to show:

- **High-quality instruction is reflected in the use of a variety of classroom teaching practices, allowing for both teacher-directed and self-regulated learning.** Although the use of a variety of classroom teaching practices is seen in every country examined, only a minority of teachers reports a comparatively diverse and frequent use of different classroom teaching practices during lessons.

- **Few teachers belong to a 'professional learning community'.** TALIS data show that whereas in many countries basic forms of co-operation among staff are common, participation in reflective inquiry and collaboration, where teachers work together on the core of their professional activities, are much less common.

- **Teachers who use more diverse teaching practices and who participate more actively in professional learning communities report higher levels of self-efficacy, and receive more feedback and appraisal on their teaching,** as well as being more involved in professional development activities outside school.

- **Participation by teachers in co-operative practices is more frequent in larger schools.** While teachers in smaller schools were on average more likely to show more frequent use of different teaching practices during lessons, participation in co-operative practices like teachers observing each other, giving feedback, and acting as a mentor, advisor or specialist is more frequent in larger schools.

- **Longer working hours are associated with frequent use of different teaching practices during lessons, and with participation in co-operative practices,** suggesting that high-quality teaching and intensive forms of co-operative professional learning can be time-consuming.

📖 *Teaching Practices and Pedagogical Innovation: Evidence from TALIS,* 2012, Chapter 6

Teachers are positive about the appraisal and feedback they receive, but in some countries a significant minority or even majority of teachers have not received any in recent years: Teachers across the different systems surveyed by TALIS tend to be positive about the appraisal and feedback they receive, reporting that on the whole it is fair and helpful for their work, and increases their job satisfaction. Approximately 13% of teachers surveyed by TALIS reported that they had received no feedback or evaluation in their current school in the previous five years; this average level rises to much higher levels in Ireland (26%), Italy (55%), Portugal (26%) and Spain (46%).

📖 *Creating Effective Teaching and Learning Environments: First Results from TALIS,* 2009, Chapter 5 and Executive Summary

Figure 2.3.

Proportion of class time spent teaching and learning, by new and experienced teachers (2008)

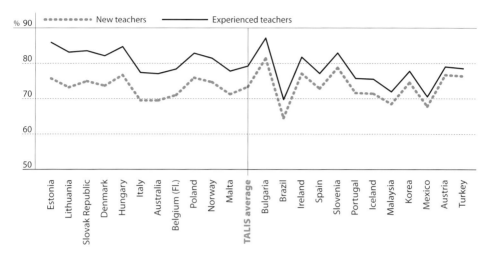

Countries are ranked in descending order based on the difference in the time reported by new teachers and experienced teachers for actual teaching and learning.
Note: All countries in this figure show statistically significant differences between new and experienced teachers.
Source: OECD, Teaching And Learning International Survey 2008.

StatLink ᵐˢᵖ http://dx.doi.org/10.1787/888932577897

New lower secondary teachers spend a smaller proportion of their time teaching than their more experienced peers: Among the teachers surveyed by TALIS on average, about three-quarters of new teachers' classroom time is spent on actual teaching and learning with a small gap between new teachers and experienced teachers. The main reason for this small gap in lost class time is the greater percentage of class time that new teachers spent on keeping order in the classroom. On average, new teachers spent slightly more time on lesson planning and slightly less time teaching students and performing administrative duties, but the magnitude of these differences is small in most countries.

📖 *The Experience from New Teachers: Results from TALIS 2008*, 2012, Chapters 2 and 5 and Executive Summary

High proportions of lower secondary teachers participate in professional development but many say that they would like more: Nearly 9 in 10 teachers surveyed by TALIS reported having taken part in a structured professional development activity in the preceding 18 months, though in Denmark, the Slovak Republic and Turkey around a quarter reported no participation during that period. Despite generally high levels of participation, more than half the teachers (55%) in the TALIS countries overall say that they would have liked more professional development, and lack of suitable opportunities is a significant factor in this.

Approximately a third of the surveyed teachers reported a high level of need for training to help them teach students with special learning needs. Other professional development priorities include teaching with ICT and dealing with difficult student behaviour.

📖 *Creating Effective Teaching and Learning Environments: First Results from TALIS,* 2009, Chapter 3 and Executive Summary

High "intended instruction hours" for those in school between the ages of 7 and 14 years-old bear no obvious association with higher academic performance at age 15: "Intended instruction hours" covers the compulsory and non-compulsory time when schools must offer teaching to school students (actual hours may vary from this, with variations too by region or type of school). Students in OECD countries are expected on average to receive an average of 6 862 hours of instruction between the ages of 7 and 14, and most of that is compulsory. Requirements vary widely among OECD countries, from 5 644 hours in Estonia to 8 664 hours in Chile (Estonia thus requires less than two-thirds instruction time compared with Chile). This while Estonia performs well on PISA, and two countries that perform particularly well – Korea and Finland – also have relatively low intended instruction hours at 5 908 and 5 753, respectively.

📖 *Education at a Glance 2012: OECD Indicators,* 2012, Indicator D1

High performance is associated with high relative time in regular lessons and moderate absolute time: The relative balance spent in regular as opposed to out-of-school learning seems to be particularly influential. In high-performing countries, the largest proportion of students' learning time (70% to 80%) happens within regular school lessons, whereas in low-performing countries, half or more of students' learning time occurs outside regular lessons. Longer hours do not by themselves bestow an advantage as in many countries long hours in regular mathematics lessons is actually associated with lower performance compared with moderate hours. As exceptions, in Korea and the partner economies Chinese Taipei and Hong Kong-China, those spending long hours learning mathematics in regular lessons perform significantly better in this subject than other students.

📖 *Quality Time for Students: Learning In and Out of School,* 2011, Chapter 4

School leadership is pivotal for the quality of schooling through creating the right organisational and educational conditions for effectiveness and improvement: A large body of research evidence on school effectiveness and improvement consistently highlights the pivotal role of leadership. It is nevertheless a complex role as leaders largely work outside the classrooms where teaching and learning takes place. Hence, instead of shaping quality directly, leaders do so by creating the right conditions for good teaching and learning through such factors as professional motivations, capacities and working environments. They are especially influential as regards four key dimensions: improving teacher quality; goal-setting, assessment and accountability; strategic resource management; and collaboration with external partners.

📖 *Improving School Leadership: Volume 1: Policy and Practice,* 2008, Chapter 1

Figure 2.4.

Total number of intended instruction hours in public institutions between the ages of 7 and 14 (2010)

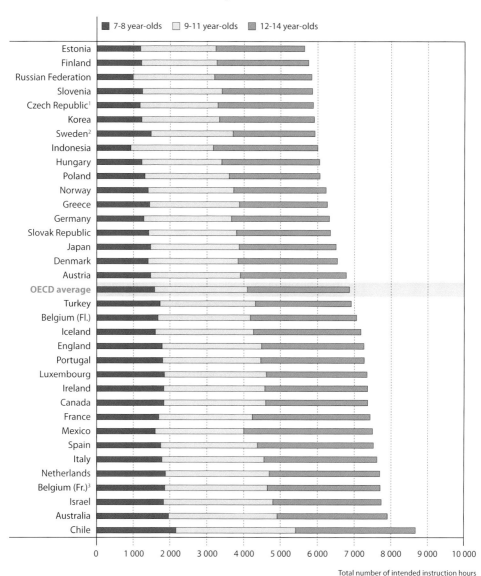

1. Minimum number of hours per year.

2. Estimated because breakdown by age is not available.

3. "12-14 year-olds" covers ages 12-13 only.

Countries are ranked in ascending order of the total number of intended instruction hours.

Source: OECD (2012), *Education at a Glance 2012: OECD Indicators,* OECD Publishing. Table D1.1. See Annex 3 for notes (*www.oecd.org/edu/eag2012*).

StatLink 🖼📈 http://dx.doi.org/10.1787/888932663511

PISA data permit the analysis of computer use in schools and at home, and how these relate to educational performance. Based on the 2009 survey data, some key findings to emerge are:

- **All students in OECD countries are now familiar with computers:** less than 1% of 15-year-old students in OECD countries declared that they had never used a computer.

- **Frequent use of computers at home is not matched by equivalent use at school:** The OECD average for 15-year-olds reporting using computers at home is 93%, compared with only 71% reporting their use in school. This indicates that the adoption of ICT for learning in schools has not kept pace with the use of ICT at home. As most students have access to a computer at school, the low level of ICT use at school most likely indicates that ICT has not yet been fully integrated into pedagogical practices.

- **There is a stronger correlation between educational performance and computer use at home than with its use in school:** In most countries, computer use at home tends to be greater than its use at school. In every country, students reporting "rare" or "no use" of computers at home score lower than their counterparts who report frequent use. But in school, more intensive computer use is not associated with better results.

- **Computer use at home is positively associated with higher navigation skills and digital reading performance, while the computer use at school is not:** After accounting for students' academic abilities, the frequency of computer use at home, particularly computer use for leisure, is positively associated with navigation skills and digital reading performance, while the frequency of computer use at school is not. These findings suggest that students are developing digital reading literacy mainly by using computers at home to pursue their interests

📖 *PISA Results 2009: Students On Line: Digital Technologies and Performance,* 2011, Executive Summary

Some countries persist with repetition of school years as common practice despite its cost – to individuals and the system alike: Among OECD countries 13% of 15-year-olds repeat at least one year either in primary or secondary school. This proportion is particularly high in France, Luxembourg, Spain, Portugal and Belgium, where it affects over 30% of students. The financial costs of grade repetition are large for both the individuals and society. Its direct costs for the school systems are very high, as they include providing an additional year of education and delaying entry into the labour market by a year: the full economic cost is up to USD 20 000 equivalent for each student who repeats a year. In Belgium, the Netherlands, Portugal and Spain the direct costs of grade repetition account for more than 8% of the annual expenditure on primary and secondary education. Schools themselves have few incentives to take into account the costs involved.

📖 *Equity and Quality in Education: Supporting Disadvantaged Students and Schools,* 2012, Chapter 2; *No More Failures: Ten Steps to Equity in Education,* 2007, Chapter 4

PISA shows that awareness of effective learning strategies is closely associated with student proficiency in reading: PISA 2009 asked students to self-report the extent to which they are aware of effective strategies to understand and summarise information. Across OECD countries, the difference in reading performance between those students who know the most about which strategies are best for summarising information and those who know the least is 107 score points. These findings underline the importance for parents, teachers and schools to provide students with the support and tools to become effective readers and learners.

📖 *PISA 2009 Results: Learning to Learn: Student Engagement, Strategies and Practices,* 2010, Chapter 2 and Policy Implications

Fifteen-year-olds across the world report their strong interest in environmental issues and identify their schooling as the most important source of knowledge about the environment: Students across the world report their strong interest in issues related to the environment. They also cite school – particularly but not only in their geography and science lessons – as the place where they learn most about the environment. Student awareness of environmental issues tends to go hand in hand with their measured level of scientific knowledge and proficiency. On the other hand, those with lower proficiency levels in environmental science tend to be more optimistic that the environment will improve in the future highlighting the important role that education can play in raising awareness.

📖 *Green at Fifteen? How 15-Year-Olds Perform in Environmental Science and Geoscience in PISA 2006,* 2009, Chapters 3 and 4

Certain countries strongly maintain the public nature of schooling by accepting neither private provision nor homeschooling: Most OECD countries report that independent (not government-dependent) private schools are permitted in their system, even if the number of students involved is usually relatively small. However, they are not permitted in the Czech Republic, Finland, the Slovak Republic and Sweden, and for the lower secondary level in Korea, too. Homeschooling is also an option in many countries, albeit under certain conditions, but is not allowed in Germany, Greece, Japan, Korea, Mexico, Spain and partner country Brazil, and not at the lower secondary level in the Czech Republic and Slovak Republic.

📖 *Education at a Glance 2010: OECD Indicators,* 2010, Indicator D5

In OECD and non-OECD G20 countries, primary and secondary education is mostly provided by public institutions: On average, 90% of primary education students in OECD countries are enrolled in public schools. The proportion is slightly smaller in secondary education, with 86% of lower secondary students and 81% of upper secondary students taught in public schools. Public and government-dependent institutions combined enrol 97% of students at the lower secondary level and 95% at the secondary level. These percentages vary widely among countries however. For example, in Indonesia 36% of lower secondary students and 50% of upper secondary students are enrolled in independent private schools.

📖 *Education at a Glance 2012: OECD Indicators,* 2012, Indicator C1

POLICY DIRECTIONS

TALIS 2008 analysis suggests the following policy implications regarding new and experienced lower secondary teachers:

- **Greater job differentiation between new and experienced teachers would improve effective teaching and learning within schools.** Reducing teaching responsibilities for new teachers would provide more time for them to develop their teaching skills at the beginning of their careers and increase effective teaching and learning in schools.

- **Appraisal and feedback are considered to be beneficial by new teachers and important for improving their teaching.** Appraisal and feedback also impact positively on job satisfaction and theQQ sense of job security among new teachers. Constructive feedback needs to be maintained so that as current new teachers mature in the profession, their job satisfaction and development needs will be met.

- **There is a need to increase the intensity of mentoring and induction programmes and ensure that these provide the much needed constructive feedback.** Mentoring and induction programmes in their current forms do not provide sufficient feedback that new teachers say they need. The evidence also shows that the greater the frequency of mentoring programmes, the greater their impact on student outcomes.

- **New teachers need support and development to improve their classroom management practices.** TALIS showed that the practical classroom skills of classroom management and dealing with problems of student discipline are identified by new teachers as difficult issues for them.

📖 *The Experience from New Teachers: Results from TALIS 2008,* 2012, Chapter 6

The quality of school leadership needs to be enhanced and it needs to be made sustainable. Four main policy levers, taken together, can improve school leadership practice:

- **Redefine school leadership responsibilities:** Leaders need to exercise a significant degree of autonomy if they are to influence quality, and policy should ensure that they have this. Policy should encourage leaders to: support, evaluate and develop teacher quality; engage in goal-setting and organisational evaluation; enhance strategic financial and human resource management; and operate more widely than within the confines of the school itself.

- **Distribute school leadership:** Leadership is strengthened, not weakened, if the responsibilities of school principals are shared effectively with other middle management and school professionals, and with school boards; policy should support and enable this to happen.

- **Develop skills for effective school leadership:** School leadership demands specific advanced competences that explicitly need development. Leadership development should contribute to the different career stages so policies should distinguish between preparation for leadership, induction programmes, and adequate in-service opportunities adapted to need and context. This career focus will also enhance attractiveness (next point).

- **Make school leadership an attractive profession:** Ensuring that the procedures for recruiting the key personnel of school leadership are highly professionalised is one important route to enhancing attractiveness. Another is to establish salaries at levels commensurate with workloads and responsibilities, compared with classroom teachers and those in other professions, and linked to local factors which influence attractiveness.

📖 *Improving School Leadership: Volume 1: Policy and Practice,* 2008, Executive Summary; *Improving School Leadership: Volume 3: The Toolkit,* 2010

School leaders can make a difference in school and student performance if they are granted the autonomy to make important decisions: School leaders need to be able to adapt teaching programs to local needs, promote teamwork among teachers, and engage in teacher monitoring, evaluation and professional development. They need discretion in setting strategic direction and must be able to develop school plans and goals and monitor progress, using data to improve practice. They also need to be able to influence teacher recruitment to improve the match between candidates and their school's needs. In addition, leadership preparation and training are central and building networks of schools to stimulate and spread innovation and to develop diverse curricula, extended services and professional support can bring substantial benefits.

📖 *Preparing Teachers and Developing School Leaders for the 21st Century: Lessons from around the World,* 2012, Chapter 1

The recent analysis of educational technology use by 15-year-olds and its relationship to achievement levels resulted in a number of policy recommendations. These include:

- **Raise awareness among educators, parents and policy makers of the consequences of increasing ICT familiarity:** Policy makers should recognise that students need technology and access to digital media for learning in 21st century societies. Teachers and the teacher education sector need to hear this clear policy message, as do parents that they also have a crucial responsibility in developing responsible attitudes to using digital media.

- **Identify and foster the development of 21st century skills and competences:** The skills and competences required by a knowledge economy are either supported or enhanced by ICT. Policy authorities should identify and conceptualise the required competence set so as to incorporate them into the educational standards that students should meet by the end of compulsory schooling.

- **Adopt holistic policy approaches to ICT in education:** Many countries have not developed holistic policies for the educational use of ICT. An overall favourable environment, the inclusion of ICT in curriculum design, and strong leadership and commitment from teachers and principals to implement ICT-rich teaching all significantly influence the use

of ICT in schools. Current policies and their results should be critically evaluated within such a holistic framework.

- **Adapt school learning environments as computer ratios improve and digital learning resources increase:** Students should be able to locate and use a computer at any time, depending on their specific individual and team assignments. Governments should provide the conditions for innovations to flourish and should assess their effects.

- **Promote greater computer use at school and experimental research on its effects:** The positive gains from computer use at home derive in part because its frequency has passed a critical threshold; it is far above the relatively marginal use often experienced at school. Governments need to create the necessary incentives for teachers to engage with ICT sufficiently that its benefits can be realised, and they should support the creation of the evidence base of "what works".

📖 *Are the New Millennium Learners Making the Grade? Technology Use and Educational Performance in PISA*, 2010, Chapter 5 and Executive Summary

Leading researchers from Europe and North America have summarised large bodies of research on learning in such a way as to be relevant to educational leaders and policy makers. The transversal conclusions that merge suggest that to be most effective a learning environment should adhere to the following "principles" and that ideally all should be present:

- **Recognise the learners as its core participants,** encourage their active engagement and develop in them an understanding of their own activity as learners.

- **Be founded on the social nature of learning** and actively encourage well-organised co-operative learning.

- Engage learning professionals who are highly **attuned to the learners' motivations and the key role of emotions** in achievement.

- **Be acutely sensitive to the individual differences** among the learners, including their prior knowledge.

- Devise programmes that **demand hard work and challenge from all without excessive overload.**

- Operate with clarity of expectations, **use assessment strategies consistent with these expectations**, and give strong emphasis on formative feedback.

- **Strongly promote "horizontal connectedness"** across areas of knowledge and subjects, as well as to the community and the wider world.

📖 *The Nature of Learning: Using Research to Inspire Practice,* 2010, Chapter 13 and Executive Summary

A recent study on the governance of complex education systems revealed that a growing number of OECD countries are moving towards augmenting school accountability measures based on test scores (school performance accountability) with measures involving multiple stakeholders (e.g. parents, students, etc). The study allowed for drawing some key recommendations to make multiple stakeholder accountability in schools work:

- **It is important to identify the right stakeholders:** The process of stakeholder identification can be heavily influenced by "stakeholder salience", that is, the ability of stakeholders to attract schools' attention, depending on their power, legitimacy and urgency vis-à-vis the school. In order to ensure that the identification of stakeholders is not limited to those most salient, schools must make efforts to involve less powerful or inactive stakeholders.

- **Build stakeholder capacity:** This is particularly important while establishing accountability relationships with weaker stakeholders who might not have the requisite knowledge and language to fully engage in the accountability processes.

- **Self-evaluation that provides real insight into schools' quality and processes:** Proper school self-evaluation requires "assessment literacy" from school leaders as well as from teachers and other professional staff. School leaders should empower staff to be involved, be open to parents and members of the local community, and be held accountable by them. They must also build bridges between teachers and educational staff and external accountability demands.

📖 "Looking Beyond the Numbers: Stakeholders and Multiple School Accountability", *OECD Education Working Papers,* No. 85, 2012

Seismic safety in schools should be recognised as an important goal and national programmes should be established on an urgent basis to assure earthquake safety of new and existing schools. The principles guiding such programmes should include:

- **Establish clear and measurable objectives for school seismic safety,** based on the level of risk which can be implemented and supported by the affected residents of communities and agencies at the local government level.

- **Define the level of the earthquake hazard** in order to facilitate the development and application of construction codes and standards.

- **Specify the desired ability of school buildings to resist earthquakes.** School buildings should be designed and constructed or retrofitted to prevent collapse, partial collapse or other failure that would endanger human life when subjected to specified levels of ground shaking and/or collateral seismic hazards.

- **Give priority to making new schools safe.** A longer timeframe will likely be needed to correct seismic weaknesses of existing school buildings.

📖 *OECD Recommendations Concerning Guidelines on Earthquake Safety in Schools, 2005; School Safety and Security: Keeping Schools Safe in Earthquakes,* 2004

References and Further Reading

Hooge, E., T. Burns and **H. Wilkoszewski** (2012), "Looking Beyond the Numbers: Stakeholders and Multiple School Accountability", *OECD Education Working Papers*, No. 85, OECD Publishing.

OECD (2004), *School Safety and Security: Keeping Schools Safe in Earthquakes*, OECD Publishing.

OECD (2005), *Teachers Matter: Attracting, Developing and Retaining Effective Teachers*, OECD Publishing.

OECD (2005), *OECD Recommendations Concerning Guidelines on Earthquake Safety in Schools*, OECD Publishing.

OECD (2007), *No More Failures: Ten Steps to Equity in Education*, 2007, OECD Publishing.

OECD (2008), *Improving School Leadership: Volume 1: Policy and Practice*, OECD Publishing.

OECD (2009), *Creating Effective Teaching and Learning Environments: First Results from TALIS*, OECD Publishing.

OECD (2009), *Green at Fifteen? How 15-Year-Olds Perform in Environmental Science and Geoscience in PISA 2006*, OECD Publishing.

OECD (2010), *Improving School Leadership: Volume 3: The Toolkit*, OECD Publishing.

OECD (2010), *Are the New Millennium Learners Making the Grade? Technology Use and Educational Performance in PISA*, OECD Publishing.

OECD (2010), *Education at a Glance 2010: OECD Indicators*, OECD Publishing.

OECD (2010), *The Nature of Learning: Using Research to Inspire Practice*, OECD Publishing.

OECD (2010), *PISA 2009 Results: Learning to Learn: Students Engagement, Strategies and Practices (Volume III)*, OECD Publishing.

OECD (2011), *PISA Results 2009: Students On Line: Digital Technologies and Performance (Volume VI)*, OECD Publishing.

OECD (2011), *Building a High-Quality Teaching Profession: Lessons from around the World*, OECD Publishing.

OECD (2011), *Quality Time for Students: Learning In and Out of School*, OECD Publishing.

OECD (2012), *Equity and Quality in Education: Supporting Disadvantaged Students and Schools*, OECD Publishing.

OECD (2012), *Preparing Teachers and Developing School Leaders for the 21st Century: Lessons from Around the World*, OECD Publishing.

OECD (2012), *The Experience from New Teachers: Results from TALIS 2008*, OECD Publishing.

OECD (2012), *Let's Read Them a Story! The Parent Factor in Education*, OECD Publishing.

OECD (2012), *Education at a Glance 2012: OECD Indicators*, OECD Publishing.

OECD (2012), *Teaching Practices and Pedagogical Innovation: Evidence from TALIS*, OECD Publishing.

3

Transitions Beyond Initial Education

The OECD has examined arrangements and policies surrounding the transitions beyond compulsory schooling. Extended education to at least completion of the upper secondary cycle is increasingly the norm right now across the OECD countries. Alongside shared patterns are marked differences on such matters as the relative proportions who engage in general or vocational study, as well as the possibilities to combine education with employment. Vocational education and training – which have tended to be neglected in countries compared with general school and university programmes, and which often do not well meet labour market needs – have been the focus of recent OECD review, with the publication Learning for Jobs. *OECD policy orientations have stressed the need to improve the existence, diversity, relevance and transparency of different pathways, and the need to integrate them into a lifelong learning perspective, while protecting those left most vulnerable as others advance to further education and employment. The OECD recently released its Skills Strategy, an integrated, cross-government strategic framework that aims to help countries to identify the strengths and weaknesses of their existing national skills pool and skills systems, benchmark them internationally, and develop policies for improvement.*

The statistical data for Israel are supplied by and under the responsibility of the relevant Israeli authorities. The use of such data by the OECD is without prejudice to the status of the Golan Heights, East Jerusalem and Israeli settlements in the West Bank under the terms of international law.

INTRODUCTION

OECD analyses have shed extensive light on the issues, arrangements and policies surrounding the transitions beyond compulsory schooling. Extended education with at least completion of the upper secondary cycle is increasingly the norm right across the OECD countries. Alongside shared patterns are marked differences on such matters as the relative proportions who engage in general or vocational study, as well as the possibilities to combine education with employment. OECD studies on guidance, information systems and qualifications have shown that there is much scope for improving transitions. Policy orientations have stressed the need to improve the existence, diversity, relevance and transparency of different pathways, while protecting those left most vulnerable as others advance to further education and employment; messages that have gained even more relevance since the onset of the economic crisis.

An earlier relative neglect of vocational education and training (VET) at the OECD has been addressed with reviews of VET policies and of systemic innovation in the VET field. Work at the secondary level and apprenticeships, encapsulated in the major report *Learning for Jobs*, has been extended towards the role of post-secondary and tertiary vocational education in paving pathways to jobs.

The OECD recently released its *Skills Strategy* – an integrated, cross-government strategic framework to help countries understand better how to invest in skills in ways to transform lives and drive economies. It aims to help countries to identify the strengths and weaknesses of their existing national skills pool and skills systems, benchmark them internationally, and develop policies for improvement. In the future, the OECD will support countries with the development and review of their skills strategies.

KEY FINDINGS

Secondary education has become the dominant experience for 17-year-olds in OECD countries: At age 17, almost 9 out of 10 young people in OECD countries are in secondary education (87%). In some it is the quasi-totality of the age group at 95% or more (Belgium, the Czech Republic, Finland, Hungary, Poland, Portugal, Slovenia and Sweden). Seventeen-year-olds in secondary education are only the minority in Mexico (49%). Not all countries have figures for 17-year-olds already in post-secondary non-tertiary education, but among those that do, Austria stands out as having a sizeable minority of this teenage group (12%) transferred to such programmes. And in some countries, a small number have already launched into tertiary education even at this young age (e.g. in Australia [5%], Canada [3%], Germany [3%], Ireland [5%], Mexico [3%], the Netherlands [7%], New Zealand [3%]).

📖 *Education at a Glance 2012: OECD Indicators*, 2012, Indicator C1

Nearly three-quarters of 18-year-olds are still in education across OECD countries (73%), with already over a fifth in post-secondary education: In certain countries, the large majority of the age group continues in secondary education at 18 years of age: 80-90% in the Czech Republic, Denmark, Iceland, Norway, the Slovak Republic and Slovenia, and over 90% in Finland (93%), Poland (91%) and Sweden (94%). In others, significant numbers have already embarked on tertiary programmes – a third or more of 18-year-olds in Belgium (36%), Greece (43%), Ireland (36%), the United States (43%), rising to close to two-thirds in Korea (65%). Over one-in-five 18-year-olds in Austria (21%) and Ireland (23%) are in non-tertiary post-secondary programmes, compared with the OECD average of 3%.

📖 *Education at a Glance 2012: OECD Indicators*, 2012, Indicator C1

Figure 3.1.

Population that has attained upper secondary education[1] (2010)

Percentage, by age group

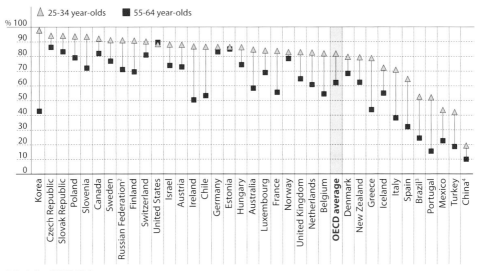

1. Excluding ISCED 3C short programmes.
2. Year of reference 2002.
3. Year of reference 2009.
4. Year of reference 2000.

Countries are ranked in descending order of the percentage of 25-34 year-olds who have attained at least an upper secondary education.

Source: OECD (2012), *Education at a Glance 2012: OECD Indicators*, OECD Publishing. Table A1.2a. See Annex 3 for notes (*www.oecd.org/edu/eag2012*).

StatLink ᴴᴵˢᴸ http://dx.doi.org/10.1787/888932661497

Enrolment rates among 15-19 year-olds in OECD countries increased by more than 10 percentage points in the past 15 years: In OECD countries, enrolment rates among 15-19 year-olds increased on average by 10.4 percentage points between 1995 and 2010. The increase was more than 20 percentage points during this period in the Czech Republic, Greece, Hungary and Turkey (despite Turkey having the largest increase in cohort size among OECD countries), and by around 15 points or more in Ireland, Mexico, Poland and Portugal.

They remained virtually unchanged in Belgium, Canada (until 2009), Germany, Israel and the Netherlands, where (except Israel), more than 85% of 15-19 year-olds were already enrolled in education, while in France, the enrolment rate among this age group decreased from 89% to 84% during this period.

📖 *Education at a Glance 2012: OECD Indicators,* 2012, Indicator C1

Completion of upper secondary education has become the norm over the past 15 years: In 1997, on average across OECD countries, the proportion of 25-64 year olds who had attained an upper secondary education amounted to only just about two-thirds (64%). By 2010, the proportion had increased by 10 percentage points (to 74%). Now only a handful of countries – Greece, Iceland, Italy, Mexico, Portugal, Spain and Turkey – have upper secondary attainment rates below 70% for 25-64 year-olds. Some of these countries have seen dramatic increases in upper secondary attainment rates from generation to generation. For example, Chile, Greece, Ireland, Italy, Korea, Portugal and Spain have all seen an increase of 30% or more from the older (55-64 year-old) to the younger (25-34 year-old) age cohorts on this measure. By contrast, it has increased only marginally, or even fallen, in countries with traditionally high levels of upper secondary attainment in previous generations. For instance, in Estonia, Germany and Norway the upper secondary attainment rate rose by less than 5 percentage points between the 55-64 year-old and 25-34 year-old age cohorts; in the United States it decreased slightly.

📖 *Education at a Glance 2012: OECD Indicators,* 2012, Indicator A1

In a reversal of the long-term historical pattern, young women are now more likely than young men to graduate from upper secondary programmes in almost all OECD countries: In all countries with available data, boys are less likely to finish upper secondary school with a diploma. On average, 74% of girls complete their upper secondary education within the stipulated time, compared with 66% of boys, a reversal from the historical trend. In Iceland and Norway, girls outnumber the boys who successfully complete upper secondary education by more than 15 percentage points. Only in Finland, Japan, Korea, the Slovak Republic and Sweden is the difference less than five percentage points, though with girls still ahead.

📖 *Education at a Glance 2012: OECD Indicators,* 2012, Indicator A2

More than eight out of ten of today's young people will complete upper secondary education over their lifetimes: Based on current patterns of graduation, 84% of today's young people will complete upper secondary education over their lifetimes; in G20 countries, some 78% of young people will. In some countries, it is not uncommon for students to graduate from upper secondary programmes after the age of 25: around 10% of upper secondary graduates in Denmark, Finland and Norway are 25 years or older, rising to 20% in Iceland, and to more than 40% in Portugal.

📖 *Education at a Glance 2012: OECD Indicators,* 2012, Indicator A2

For young adults across OECD countries, 7 years can now be expected to be spent in education between the ages of 15 and 29: Synthesising current enrolment patterns for young people in their latter teens and twenties, not far off half (7.0 years) of the 15 years between mid-teenage years and the end of their twenties will now be spent in education. Eight years or more of this age span is spent in education in Denmark, Finland, Iceland (women), Luxembourg (women), the Netherlands, Slovenia and Sweden (women). The "educational expectancy" of this transition age group tends to be longer among young women than young men though there are exceptions to this (Germany, Japan, Korea, Mexico, the Netherlands, Switzerland and Turkey). In Iceland, Italy, Norway, Slovenia and Sweden, a young woman can expect on average to spend a year longer or more in education than a young man.

📖 *Education at a Glance 2012: OECD Indicators,* 2012, Indicator C5

Certain countries do not mix education with employment together for young adults: How the average 7 years in education between the age of 15 and 29 will be experienced – in particular, whether it will include being in employment status while also in education – varies sharply from country to country. There are some cases where these years will be primarily devoted to education without mixing this with employment status. For instance, less than 12 months on average for men and women combined from age 15 to 29 are counted as being in both education and employment in the following countries: Belgium (0.6 in the total 7.0 years in education between these ages), France (0.9 in 6.6), Greece (0.4 in 6.6), Hungary (0.3 in 7.2), Italy (0.4 in 6.8), Japan (0.8 in 6.2, up to the age of 24 years), Korea (0.8 in 6.8), Luxembourg (0.7 in 8.2), Portugal (0.6 in 6.5), the Slovak Republic (0.9 in 6.9), Spain (0.7 in 6.0) and Turkey (0.8 in 4.7).

📖 *Education at a Glance 2012: OECD Indicators,* 2012, Indicator C5

In other countries, being in "education" means being in employment as well for many young people: There are other countries with a "mixed model" where an important part of the years in education are simultaneously in employment, including on work study programmes. In some countries indeed, more than half of this time in education will have the double status combining it with employment (Australia, Denmark, Iceland, the Netherlands and Switzerland).

📖 *Education at a Glance 2012: OECD Indicators,* 2012, Indicator C5

A relatively even balance between students enrolled in upper secondary general and vocational programmes across OECD countries as a whole hides very large differences across countries: Just over half of upper secondary level students (54%) are in "general" and the others are in pre-vocational and vocational tracks. Over 65% are in "general" tracks in Canada, Chile, Estonia, Greece, Hungary, Iceland, Japan, Korea, Mexico, New Zealand and the United Kingdom, and in the partner countries Argentina and Brazil. On the other hand, over 65% are in the vocational tracks in Austria, Belgium, the Czech Republic, Finland, the Netherlands, the Slovak Republic and Switzerland.

📖 *Education at a Glance 2012: OECD Indicators,* 2012, Indicator C1

In general, vocational education and training (VET) has been neglected: VET can play a central role in preparing young people for work, developing the skills of adults and responding to the labour-market needs of the economy. Despite this, VET has tended to be marginalised in policy discussions, often overshadowed by the increasing emphasis on general academic education and the role of schools in preparing students for university education. It is also often regarded as of low status by students and the general public. There are very limited data on VET available, especially data that can reliably be compared across countries.

📖 *Learning for Jobs,* 2010, Summary and Policy Messages and Chapter 1

Figure 3.2.
**Percentage of 15-19 year-olds not in education and unemployed
or not in the labour force (2010)**

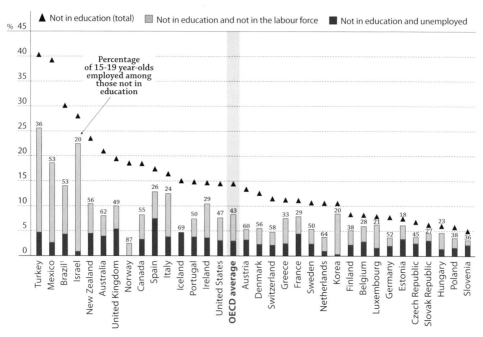

1. Year of reference 2009.

Countries are ranked in descending order of the percentage of 15-19 year-olds not in education.

Source: OECD (2012), *Education at a Glance 2012: OECD Indicators,* OECD Publishing. Table C5.2a. See Annex 3 for notes (www.oecd.org/edu/eag2012).

StatLink ᓆᓐ http://dx.doi.org/10.1787/888932663340

While strong vocational programmes increase competitiveness, many programmes fail to meet labour market needs: Many of the unskilled jobs which existed in OECD countries a generation ago are fast disappearing and OECD countries need to compete on the quality of goods and services they provide. This calls for a labour force well-equipped with middle-level trade, technical and professional skills usually delivered through vocational programmes alongside the high skills associated with university education. But VET systems face major challenges and vocational programmes for young people, often rooted in education institutions, tend to develop their own dynamic and can become too easily separated from the fast-changing world of modern economies.

📖 *Learning for Jobs,* 2010, Summary and Policy Messages and Chapter 2

Across OECD countries about one in six young adults is neither employed, nor in education and training: After several years of decline, the proportion of 15-29 year-olds that are neither employed, nor in education or training - the "NEET" population – has increased rapidly since the outset of the economic crisis, resulting in a proportion of 16% across OECD countries in 2010. This proportion varies widely across countries, however. At one side of the spectrum are Ireland, Israel, Italy, Mexico, Spain and Turkey where more that 20% of young adults are not in education or employed, while in Luxembourg, the Netherlands, Norway, Slovenia and Switzerland this is less than 10%. This increase reflects the hardship facing young people as a result of the global recession.

📖 *Education at a Glance 2012: OECD Indicators,* 2012, Editorial and Indicator C5

In rapidly-changing economies, career guidance has become more critical but it suffers serious weaknesses in many OECD countries: Young people face a sequence of complex choices over a lifetime of learning and work; helping them to make these decisions is the task of career guidance. But in many countries, career guidance suffers from serious weaknesses. Too often those offering guidance are inadequately acquainted with labour market issues; guidance services can be fragmented, underresourced and reactive, so that those who most need guidance risk failing to obtain it; many guidance personnel are based in education institutions and may give partial, pro-academic advice; relevant labour market information is too often not available or not readily comprehensible; and the evidence base on "what works" in career guidance is generally weak.

📖 *Learning for Jobs,* 2010, Summary and Policy Messages and Chapter 3

Box 3.1. **Education and economic crisis**

The economic crisis has affected labour markets in a number of ways. Part-time work has increased, average actual hours worked by the full-time employed have decreased and the number of employees with temporary contracts has decreased in European countries. While the overall unemployment rate among the OECD countries increased by 2.4 percentage points between 2008 and 2010 (from 6.1% to 8.5%), the extent of the increase varies with age and level of education.

...

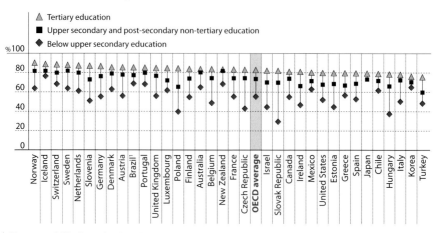

**Percentage of 25-64 year-olds in employment,
by educational attainment level (2010)**

How to read this chart: The chart shows a positive relationship between education and employment. The likelihood of being in employment increases with higher levels of education. Individuals with tertiary education have the highest employment rate, compared to those with upper secondary education and below upper secondary education. However, the magnitude of this employment advantage varies across countries.

1. Year of reference 2009.
Countries are ranked in descending order of the employment rate of tertiary-educated individuals.
Source: OECD (2012), *Education at a Glance 2012: OECD Indicators,* OECD Publishing. Table A7.3a. See Annex 3 for notes (*www.oecd.org/edu/eag2012*).

StatLink ᴍ◆ http://dx.doi.org/10.1787/888932662029

The youth population has been most affected. The unemployment rates for 15-24 year-olds increased by 4 percentage points, from 12.7% to 16.7% between 2008 and 2010. The labour market has become more selective and the lack of relevant skills and experience brings a higher risk of unemployment for recent entrants. The extent of the risk decreases as level of education increases.

Having more education has helped people avoid unemployment and stay employed during the economic crisis. Unemployment rates among 25-64 year-olds without an upper secondary education rose by 3.8 percentage points between 2008 and 2010, whereas for those with an upper secondary education, the unemployment rate increased by 2.7 percentage points and among tertiary-educated graduates, the rate rose by 1.4 percentage points over this time. The increase in the unemployment rate was particularly evident among men without an upper secondary education compared to women with the same level of education (4.3 percentage points increase compared with 2.3 percentage points).

In most countries, there is a drop at upper secondary level in the students with special needs and receiving additional resources, compared with the primary and lower secondary levels: For students with disabilities, a median of 1.6% receive additional funding at this level as against 3.3% for lower secondary. (The only exception to the drop between levels among the countries with data is England.) Similarly, the proportion getting additional financial resources specifically for learning difficulties is lower at the upper than the lower secondary level, again with the exception of England. For those recognised as having disadvantages and being thereby entitled to additional resources, there is again a drop between the two levels in most countries, with only the Slovak Republic showing a marginal increase from lower to upper secondary.

📖 *Students with Disabilities, Learning Difficulties and Disadvantages: Policies, Statistics and Indicators,* 2008, Chapter 4

There is an important gap between the developed cognitive capacity in mid-teenagers ("high horsepower") and their emotional maturity ("poor steering"): The insights provided by neuroscience on adolescence are especially important as this is the period when so much takes place in an individual's educational career. The secondary phase of education brings key decisions to be made with long-lasting consequences regarding personal, educational and career options. At this time, young people are already well-developed in terms of cognitive capacity ("high horsepower") but they are immature ("poor steering"), not just because of inexperience, but because of under-developed neurological emotional development.

📖 *Understanding the Brain: The Birth of a Learning Science,* 2007, Conclusions and Future Prospects

POLICY DIRECTIONS

The *OECD Skills Strategy* provides an integrated, cross-government strategic framework aimed to help countries understand more about how to invest in skills to help transform better skills into better jobs, economic growth and social inclusion. To this end, the first main policy lever to address is to **develop relevant skills:**

- **Gather and use information about changing skills demand to guide skills development.** More high-level skills are needed than ever before. Changes in skills demand have to be identified, articulated and translated into relevant curricula and programmes.

- **Engage social partners** in designing and delivering curricula and education and training programmes.

- **Ensure that education and training programmes are of high-quality.** Institutions need to be governed by a clear quality assurance framework that serves both accountability and improvement purposes, and that combines internal and external evaluation without imposing an excessive administrative burden.

- **Promote equity by ensuring access to, and success in, quality education for all.** Investing in high-quality, early childhood education and initial schooling, the provision of financial support targeted at disadvantaged students and schools later in life and second-chance options should all be considered.

- **Ensure that costs are shared and tax systems do not discourage investment in learning.** Employers can create a climate that supports learning, and governments can design financial incentives and favourable tax policies that encourage individuals and employers to invest in post-compulsory education and training.

- **Maintain a long-term perspective on skills development,** even during economic crises.

- **Facilitate entry for skilled migrants.** Formal recruitment channels, including for low-skilled migration, might be needed to close skills gaps.

- **Design policies that encourage international students to remain after their studies.** Several OECD countries have eased their immigration policies to allow international students to work during their studies and encourage them to remain after their studies to work. This practice allows these countries to make better use of this important source of skills.

- **Make it easier for skilled migrants to return to their country of origin.** Migration flows can have a positive impact on the stock of human capital in countries of origin: returning migrants bring back knowledge and experience as well as business links that are of use to their home country. To reap these advantages, countries can facilitate and encourage return migration.

- **Promote cross-border skills policies by investing in skills abroad and encourage cross-border higher education.** An increasing number of employers operate internationally and must therefore derive their skills from both local sources and the global talent pool.

📖 *Better Skills, Better Jobs, Better Lives: A Strategic Approach to Skills Policies,* 2012

The second main lever is to **activate skills supply,** encouraging people to offer their skills and to retain skilled people on the labour market:

- **Identify inactive individuals and the reasons for their inactivity.** Integrating under-represented groups into the labour force has great potential to increase the skills base.

- **Create the financial incentives to make work pay.** Childcare services, tax and benefit systems should be designed so that working is more beneficial than not working.

- **Dismantle non-financial barriers to participation in the labour force,** with employers, trade unions and government working in concert.

- **Discourage early retirement.** To keep older workers in the labour market, many countries have eliminated early retirement schemes, increased the official pensionable age and corrected distorted financial incentives to retire early. Lifelong learning and targeted training, especially in mid-career, can improve employability in later life and discourage early withdrawal from the labour market.

- **Staunch the brain drain.** Experience has shown that the best way to prevent brain drain is to provide incentives to stay, including by improving labour-market conditions locally, rather than by imposing coercive measures to prevent emigration.

📖 *Better Skills, Better Jobs, Better Lives: A Strategic Approach to Skills Policies,* 2012

The third lever is to **put skills to effective use,** creating a better match between people's skills and job requirements:

- **Help employers to make better use of their employees' skills.** Government support schemes, especially for those with low skill levels, are often necessary to address under-skilling and to achieve an optimal match between workers' skills and job requirements.

- **Provide better information about the skills needed and available.** Quality career guidance is a critical part of any skills strategy. Coherent and easy-to-interpret qualifications help employers understand the skills held by potential employees, facilitating recruitment and matching.

- **Facilitate internal mobility among local labour markets.** Reducing costs and other barriers associated with internal mobility helps employees to find suitable jobs and helps employers to find suitable workers.

- **Help economies move up the value-added chain**. Government programmes can influence both employer competitiveness strategies and product-market strategies, which determine in what markets the company competes.

- **Stimulate the creation of more high-skilled and high value-added jobs**. By fostering competition for goods and services, policy can promote productive activities that contribute to stronger economic growth and the creation of more productive and rewarding jobs. Education institutions focusing on new technologies and innovation can also help develop the skills for future economies.

- **Foster entrepreneurship**. Entrepreneurs create new jobs and increase skill demand but they are made, not born. Education and training institutions have a role here in training students to identify opportunities, turn them into successful ventures, and recognise and respond to obstacles.

- **Tackle unemployment and help young people to gain a foothold in the labour market.** In many countries, young people struggle to enter the labour market and to find stable jobs that pay a living wage and offer good career prospects. Successful entry into the labour market at the beginning of a professional career has a profound influence on later working life.

📖 *Better Skills, Better Jobs, Better Lives: A Strategic Approach to Skills Policies,* 2012

The recent VET study has synthesised wide-ranging analysis and review into five key recommendations. These include:

- **Provide the right mix of skills for the labour market:** Provide a mix of VET training places that reflect both student preferences and employer needs, and share the costs of doing so between government, employers and individuals according to who will benefit.

Engage employers and unions in curriculum development to ensure that the skills taught correspond to those needed in the modern workplace while also ensuring that the VET fosters generic, transferable skills and that students in vocational programmes have adequate numeracy and literacy skills.

- **Reform career guidance to deliver well-informed career advice for all:** Develop a coherent career guidance profession, independent from psychological counselling and well-informed by labour market information. Recognise the importance of guidance by resourcing and evaluating it adequately, and ensure objective and abundant information about careers and courses, including through partnerships with employers.

- **Recruit sufficient numbers of teachers and trainers, and ensure they are well-acquainted with modern employment needs and are pedagogically prepared:** Promote flexible pathways of recruitment and facilitate the entry of those with industry skills into the VET teacher workforce. Provide appropriate pedagogical preparation for trainers, adapted to the learning being provided. Encourage part-time working and interchange between VET institutions and industry, so that vocational teachers can update their knowledge, and trainers in firms spend time in VET institutions to enhance their pedagogical skills.

- **Make full use of workplace learning:** Make substantial use of workplace training in initial VET, ensuring that the system encourages participation by both employers and students, and that the training is of good quality, (with effective quality assurance and a clear contractual framework for apprenticeships). Sustain workplace training and respond to increased demand for full-time VET during the difficult economic climate.

- **Support the VET system by engaging stakeholders and promoting transparency:** Systematically engage with employers, trade unions and other key stakeholders in VET policy and provision and qualification frameworks, strengthening quality assurance and adopting national assessment frameworks to underpin consistent quality. Strengthen data on the labour market outcomes of VET, and the institutional capacity to use that data.

📖 *Learning for Jobs,* 2010, Chapters 2-6 and Executive Summary

A systematic approach to facilitating the school-to-work transition of young adults is urgent: Effective preparation for work entails success in academic courses, the acquisition of strong generic work skills – from punctuality and effort to being an effective team member – and technical competence in the job-specific skills needed to do the entry-level work in careers that pay well. Therefore, beyond the development of young people's academic skills and knowledge, a strong school-to-work transition system needs to be in place. Workplace training makes up an essential part of such a system.

📖 *Lessons from PISA for the United States; Strong Performers and Successful Reformers in Education,* 2011, Chapter 11

Recognise the gap between the cognitive capacity and emotional maturity in teenagers to avoid definitive choices: The gap between intellectual and emotional capacity cannot imply that important choices should simply be delayed until adulthood when the gap closes. It does suggest, with the additional powerful weight of neurological evidence, that the options taken should not take the form of definitively closing doors.

📖 *Understanding the Brain: The Birth of a Learning Science,* 2007, Chapter 2

References and Further Reading

OECD (2007), *Understanding the Brain: The Birth of a Learning Science*, OECD Publishing.

OECD (2008), *Students with Disabilities, Learning Difficulties and Disadvantages: Policies, Statistics and Indicators*, OECD Publishing.

OECD (2010), *Learning for Jobs*, OECD Reviews of Vocational Education and Training, OECD Publishing.

OECD (2011), *Lessons from PISA for the United States,* Strong Performers and Successful Reformers in Education, OECD Publishing.

OECD (2012), *Better Skills, Better Jobs, Better Lives: A Strategic Approach to Skills Policies,* OECD Publishing.

OECD (2012), *Education at a Glance 2012: OECD Indicators*, OECD Publishing.

Higher Education

Countries have shared the very rapid expansion of higher or tertiary education, which means that instead of this being an experience enjoyed by a privileged minority, it has now become even the majority experience of each new cohort. There are broad trends visible across the OECD – for instance, the growing international tertiary education market and the greater formalisation of quality assurance. Despite rising costs for the individual, tertiary education remains a primarily public enterprise in most countries. There has been prominent OECD work on higher education, including on internationalisation, a major review of tertiary education, the regional role of higher education institutions (HEIs), the future of higher education, and feasibility work on the Assessment of Higher Education Learning Outcomes (AHELO). "Supporting Quality Teaching in Higher Education" *has identified long-term improvement factors for teaching staff, decision-making bodies and institutions. Work on the transition opportunities of young adults with disabilities into tertiary education and employment has showed the progress made in recent years and identified areas for further progress. Policy orientations include the need to develop and work towards strategic visions, to ensure that quality assurance serves both improvement and accountability purposes, and to use cost sharing between the state and students as the principle to shape the sector's funding.*

The statistical data for Israel are supplied by and under the responsibility of the relevant Israeli authorities. The use of such data by the OECD is without prejudice to the status of the Golan Heights, East Jerusalem and Israeli settlements in the West Bank under the terms of international law.

INTRODUCTION

Countries share the very rapid expansion of higher or tertiary education, which means that instead of this being an experience enjoyed by a privileged minority, it has now become even the majority experience of each new cohort. There are other broad trends visible across the OECD – for instance, the growing international tertiary education market and the greater formalisation of quality assurance. A major review of tertiary education was completed in 2008 and published in two volumes. The feasibility study for the international Assessment of Higher Education Learning Outcomes (AHELO) is assessing learning outcomes internationally. Work on "Supporting Quality Teaching in Higher Education" highlights effective quality initiatives, promotes reflection and has identified long-term improvement factors for teaching staff, decision-making bodies and institutions. Reviews of higher education in regions and cities are showing the benefits of stronger interaction and engagement between institutions and local actors to reinforce social and economic development.

There has been long-running work on internationalisation of higher education at the OECD, including statistical development and analysis, policy evaluation, and the formulation of the OECD/UNESCO *Guidelines for Quality Provision in Cross-border Higher Education*. Work on "University Futures" has identified scenarios for the future, and examined trends on globalisation, demography and technology in higher education. *Pathways for Disabled Students to Tertiary Education and Employment* investigated the progress made in recent years while identifying further areas of work to encourage transitions into tertiary education and employment for all students.

Policy orientations emerging from this large body of analysis include the need to develop and work towards strategic visions, to ensure that quality assurance serves both improvement and accountability purposes, and to use cost-sharing between the state and students as the principle to shape the sector's funding.

KEY FINDINGS

Many more young adults are now in education – mostly tertiary education – compared with 15 years ago, accounting for a more than a quarter of 20-29 year-olds: In 2010 on average 27% of young adults aged 20-29 in OECD countries were enrolled in education, most of whom were in tertiary education, with 30% or more in Australia, Belgium, Denmark, Finland, Germany, Greece, Iceland, Korea, the Netherlands, New Zealand, Slovenia and Sweden. In contrast, only Denmark had 30% of 20-29 year-olds enrolled in education in 1995. From 1995 to 2010, enrolment rates among 20-29 year-olds increased by 10.1 percentage points across OECD countries, and doubled or more during this time in the Czech Republic, Greece, Hungary, Korea and Turkey. Entry rates to tertiary education went up by nearly 25 percentage points across the OECD since 1995, and by 30 points or more in Australia, Austria, the Czech Republic, Iceland, Korea, Poland, the Slovak Republic, Slovenia and the United States.

📖 *Education at a Glance 2012: OECD Indicators,* 2012, Indicators C1 and C3

More than six out of ten young adults in OECD countries will participate in university-level education at some stage of their lives based on current patterns of entry: Participation rates in tertiary education of over 50% for a single age cohort have become the benchmark for OECD countries, with 62% for countries overall. (This refers to "net entry rates" which are calculated as the proportion in a synthetic age cohort who go into university-type education at some point in their lives based on current enrolment patterns.) For some countries such entry rates are substantially higher again: 80% or more can expect to enter university-type programmes (tertiary-type A alone) in Australia, Iceland, New Zealand, Poland and Portugal.

📖 *Education at a Glance 2012: OECD Indicators*, 2012, Indicators C3

Figure 4.1.
Younger and older working-age adults having attained tertiary education (2010)
Percentage, by age group

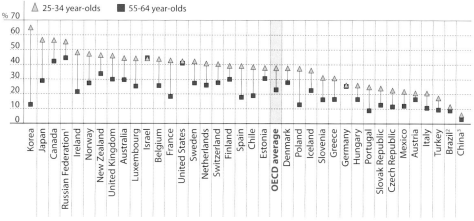

1. Year of reference 2002.
2. Year of reference 2009.
3. Year of reference 2000.
Countries are ranked in descending order of the percentage of 25-34 year-olds who have attained tertiary education.
Source: OECD (2012), *Education at a Glance 2012: OECD Indicators*, OECD Publishing. Table A1.3a. See Annex 3 for notes (*www.oecd.org/edu/eag2012*).

StatLink ᵃᵍᶦₚ http://dx.doi.org/10.1787/888932661478

The number of people with a tertiary degree has grown rapidly in OECD countries over the past decade - and even more rapidly in the non-OECD G20 countries: In 2010, there were an estimated 66 million 25-34 year-olds with a tertiary degree in OECD countries compared with 51 million ten years earlier, an increase of approximately 30%. For non-OECD G20 countries, this increase was even more marked as in 2000 there were 39 million 25-34 year-olds with a tertiary degree compared with an estimated 64 million ten years later. If this trend continues, by 2020 the number of 25-34 year-olds from Argentina, Brazil, China, India, Indonesia,

the Russian Federation, Saudi Arabia and South Africa with a higher education degree will be almost 40% higher than the number from all OECD countries put together. The strong demand for employees in "knowledge economy" fields suggests that the global labour market can continue to absorb the increased supply of highly-educated individuals.

📖 *"How Is the Global Talent Pool Changing?", Education Indicators in Focus,* No. 5, 2012

Figure 4.2.
Proportion of boys and girls planning a career in engineering or computing (2010)

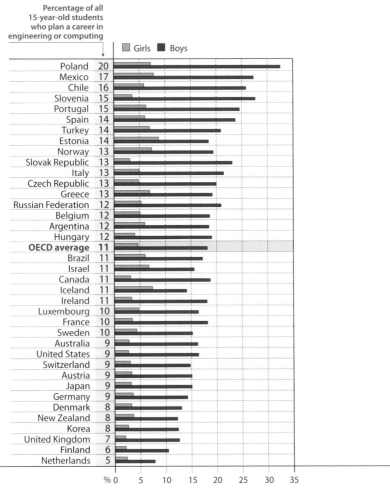

Countries are ranked in descending order of the percentage of all 15-year-old students who plan a career in engineering or computing (including architecture).
Source: OECD, *PISA 2006 Database.* OECD (2012), *Education at a Glance 2012: OECD Indicators,* OECD Publishing. Table A4.2. See Annex 3 for notes (*www.oecd.org/edu/eag2012*).

StatLink 🛰 http://dx.doi.org/10.1787/888932661763

A third of today's young students are planning a science-related career and just over one in ten in engineering and computing: PISA 2009 shows that a third of 15-year-old students across OECD countries expect to work in a science-related career as young adults, with hardly any difference between girls and boys. For those students planning a career in computing and engineering, an average of 11.3% of 15-year-olds across OECD countries, there are considerable gender differences – fewer than 5% of girls but 18% of boys expect to be working in engineering and computing, and this despite that girls in many countries have caught up with or even surpassed boys in science proficiency. Even among the top-performing girls in science few expect to enter engineering and computing.

📖 *Education at a Glance 2012: OECD Indicators,* 2012, Indicator A4

Though still a small minority across OECD countries, the number of doctoral graduates has grown considerably in the past decade with an average growth of 5% per year: Doctoral graduates obtain the highest level of formal education, and are typically trained as researchers. As such, they are important to creating and diffusing knowledge in society. In 2010, on average across OECD countries, an estimated 1.6% of young people graduated from advanced research programmes, compared to 1.0% in 2000. This increase in the past decade represents an annual growth rate of 5%. At this level, the graduation rate for women (1.5%) is lower than that of men (1.7%). Some countries promote doctoral education, particularly for international students: in Germany and Switzerland, graduation from doctoral programmes is high compared with the OECD average, at more than 2.5% of young people.

📖 *Education at a Glance 2012: OECD Indicators,* 2012, Indicator A3

Nearly a third of university students fail to graduate and such "dropout" is higher still in non-university tertiary programmes: On average across the 23 OECD countries for which data are available, some 30% of university (tertiary-type A) students fail to successfully complete the programmes they undertake. Completion rates differ widely. The countries where over three-quarters of university students complete the programme are Australia (80%), Denmark (82%), Japan (93%), Korea (84%), followed by Portugal (86%), Spain (79%), the United Kingdom (81%) and partner country the Russian Federation (80%). In contrast, in Mexico, New Zealand, Sweden and the United States less than six in ten of those who enter go on to complete (though for Sweden it includes those enrolled in single courses who do not intend to do the full programme). The non-completion rate in vocational, non-university programmes stands even higher than in university-type programmes at 38%, and is highest in New Zealand and the United States at around two-thirds, and in Portugal at over 80%.

📖 *Education at a Glance 2010: OECD Indicators,* 2010, Indicator A4

Nearly a quarter of educational expenditure is for tertiary education, accounting for 2% or more of GDP in some countries: Tertiary education accounts for nearly a quarter of expenditure on educational institutions on average in OECD countries, or 1.6% of GDP. Differences in the size of systems, pathways available to students, programme durations, and the organisation of teaching, mean that there are large differences between countries in

the levels which they spend on higher education. For instance, Canada, Chile, Korea and the United States spend between 2.4% and 2.6% of their GDP on tertiary institutions, while some countries devote less than 1% of GDP to tertiary education, the Slovak Republic (0.9%) and partner countries Brazil (0.8%), Indonesia (0.7%) and South Africa (0.6%).

📖 *Education at a Glance 2012: OECD Indicators,* 2012, Indicator B2

Tertiary education is still predominantly a public enterprise in the OECD area: There has been no general decline in enrolments, funding or public funding in public tertiary education in OECD countries. Except for Japan and Korea, tertiary education is still predominantly a public enterprise: the private for profit sector is still marginal in the large majority of countries, and even more so for advanced research programmes. At the time of writing, tertiary education institutions had not faced a major decline in public funding either; instead, their budgets have increased over recent years, in most cases per student as well as in total. Students and their households have nevertheless felt serious changes as they contribute more to the expenditures of tertiary education institutions than they used to. In most countries, however, tertiary education is still significantly publicly subsidised.

📖 *Higher Education to 2030, Volume 2, Globalisation,* 2009, Chapter 9

In the past decade, private funding for tertiary education increased by more than 7 percentage points across OECD countries, and by 10 percentage points or more in some: Across the 25 OECD countries with comparable data, the proportion of private funding for tertiary education increased from nearly 23% to 30% in the decade up to 2009. An increase in the proportion of private funding for tertiary education was seen in 18 out of the 25 countries, and it grew by as much as 20% or more in some countries (Portugal, the Slovak Republic and the United Kingdom). Only Canada, Iceland, Korea, Poland, and the United States experienced a decline in this over the decade.

📖 *Education at a Glance 2012: OECD Indicators,* 2012, Indicator B3

There has been more than a fivefold increase in foreign students since the mid-1970s, highly concentrated in a small number of destination countries: In the 1990s, there was a sharp increase in the international mobility of students and teachers, educational programmes and higher education institutions which has continued since. The number of foreign students stood at around 0.8 million worldwide in 1975 and had risen to an estimated 4.1 million by 2010. Foreign students are highly concentrated in a few countries as almost half go to the top five destination countries (the United States, the United Kingdom, Germany, France and Australia), with another 14% accounted by the next four (Canada [5%], Japan [3%], the Russian Federation [4%] and Spain [2%]). Foreign students make up around 15% or more of the tertiary student body in Australia (21.2%), Austria (15.4%), Luxembourg (41.4%), New Zealand (14.2%), Switzerland (15.4%) and the United Kingdom (16.0%). Nevertheless, the fastest growing destination regions are Latin America and the Caribbean, Oceania and Asia, mirroring university internationalisation in a growing set of countries.

📖 *Education at a Glance 2012: OECD Indicators,* 2012, Indicator C4

Figure 4.3.

Distribution of foreign students in tertiary education, by country of destination (2010)

Percentage of foreign tertiary students reported to the OECD who are enrolled in each country of destination

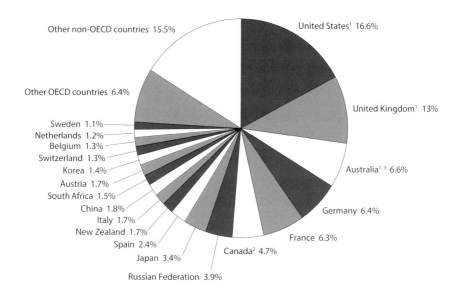

1. Data relate to international students defined on the basis of their country of residence.

2. Year of reference 2009.

3. Student stocks are derived from different sources; therefore, results should be interpreted with some caution.

Source: OECD (2012), *Education at a Glance 2012: OECD Indicators*, OECD Publishing and UNESCO Institute for Statistics for most data on non-OECD destinations. Tables C4.4 and C4.7, available on line. See Annex 3 for notes (*www.oecd.org/edu/eag2012*).

StatLink ⇲ http://dx.doi.org/10.1787/888932663188

Despite the major demographic changes taking place in OECD countries, the evolution of the academic workforce is not primarily a reflection of wider demographic trends: The age pyramid of academic staff reflects less the ageing of populations in general and more of an employment system in higher education whose hallmark is permanence with efforts to maintain relatively fixed student teacher ratios. Similarly, the changing composition of academic staff reflects less general demographic developments and more the diversification of the profession, and the restructuring of relationships between academics and their institutions.

📖 *Higher Education to 2030, Volume 1, Demography,* 2008, Chapters 3 and 4

Higher education institutions face four main challenges in managing internationalisation:

- **Cultural understanding:** Teaching and learning within different contexts and conditions can pose major challenges of cultural understanding, though differences can be advantageous if forward-looking and accurate management strategies are adopted.

- **The management of internationalisation:** Internationalisation is one of the significant components of higher education management today, and may well become still more in the near future. HE institutions need a specific strategy on internationalisation as well as up-to-date management. Internationalisation affects research, teaching, and social responsibility, all of which fall within the realm of higher education management and may need well-defined strategies to meet the challenges posed by internationalisation.

- **Regulative frameworks:** There may be contractual and legal obstacles between institutions and between countries that make collaboration difficult, e.g. regarding intellectual property and the ethics of research, or the quality standards of HE institutional operations. Despite the international networks of associations and institutions dealing with internationalisation, up to now it has progressed primarilty through institutions' individual initiatives, needs and interests.

- **Funding:** Internationalising higher education is not cost-free, and countries and institutions are not on an equal footing regarding the funding available for internationalisation. Institutions might be purely tuition-driven, others motivated by priorities set by government, or wanting to attract the best and the brightest. Funding should reflect both government and institutional needs to strike a balance between competition and cooperation.

📖 *IMHE Focus: Approaches to Internationalisation and their Implications for Strategic Management and Institutional Practice,* 2012

The OECD/UNESCO *Guidelines for Quality Provision in Cross-border Higher Education* emphasise six objectives: 1) the inclusion of cross-border higher education in the regulatory frameworks of countries, 2) the coverage of all forms of cross-border higher education, 3) student and customer protection, 4) transparency in procedures, 5) information access and dissemination, 6) collaboration. A recent survey of compliance with the *Guidelines* among OECD countries and some non-members found:

- **Four of the six objectives tend to be met.** Countries have regulatory frameworks or arrangements in place, cover different forms of cross-border higher education comprehensively, are transparent in their procedures, and are engaged in national and international collaboration. The main compliance weaknesses regard easy access to information and the level of student and customer protection.

- **OECD countries conform to 72% of the main recommendations made to governments, tertiary education institutions, and quality assurance and accreditation agencies.** The level of compliance decreases to 67% when recommendations to student bodies are included, but the level of missing information also increases significantly.

- **Tertiary education institutions are the stakeholders that most follow the *Guidelines* recommendations with an average compliance of 80%.** Governments and quality assurance and accreditation bodies comply on average with 76% and 61% of the

Guidelines, respectively. Student bodies only conform to 51% of the recommendations – with the caveat that information about their activities is scant in the survey responses.

📖 *"Guidelines for Quality Provision in Cross-border Higher Education: Where Do We Stand?", OECD Working Papers,* No. 70, 2012

Inclusive policies have increased access to tertiary education for students with disabilities, but with transition still a concern: More flexible learning environments that can be adapted to the diversity of educational needs, the reduction of dropout rates, and quality assurance policies have all helped to increase the number of students with disabilities aspiring to tertiary education. This positive trend is also a direct result of the strategies adopted by upper secondary schools and tertiary education institutions to build pathways to tertiary education and prepare upper secondary school students to cope with the demands of the transition to adulthood. Despite the progress made, young adults with disabilities generally have a more difficult transition to tertiary education than other young adults. Those students with a sensory, motor or mental impairment or psychological problems face particular challenges.

📖 *Inclusion of Students with Disabilities in Tertiary Education and Employment,* 2011, Chapters 1-4

POLICY DIRECTIONS

While recognising differences of culture and approach in national tertiary education systems, there are a number of common main elements that underpin sound planning and policy making:

- **Develop and articulate a vision for tertiary education:** Countries should as a priority develop a comprehensive and coherent vision for the future of tertiary education, to guide the medium- and long-term in harmony with national social and economic objectives. Ideally, it should result from a systematic review and entail a clear statement of strategic aims.

- **Establish sound instruments for steering towards and implementing that vision:** Tertiary education authorities need to develop their review and monitoring capacity for the system as a whole as opposed to the standard instruments of institutional administration. Within the overall vision, steering instruments need to establish a balance between institutional autonomy and public accountability. Allowing the play of student choice can improve quality and efficiency.

- **Strengthen the ability of institutions to align with the national tertiary education strategy:** Institutions should be encouraged to develop an outward focus, including via external representation on their governing bodies, and be required to establish strategic plans. The national policy framework should give institutions the means to manage their wider responsibilities effectively.

📖 *Tertiary Education for the Knowledge Society: Volume 1,* 2008, Chapter 3

Lessons drawn from OECD review about the implementation of tertiary education reforms suggest that it should:

- **Recognise the different viewpoints of stakeholders** through iterative policy development.
- **Allow for bottom-up initiatives** to come forward as proposals by independent committees.
- **Establish ad-hoc independent committees** to initiate tertiary education reforms and involve stakeholders.
- **Use pilots and experimentation.**
- **Favour incremental reforms** over comprehensive overhauls unless there is wide public support for change.
- **Avoid reforms with concentrated costs and diffused benefits.**
- **Identify potential losers** from tertiary education reform and build in compensatory mechanisms.
- **Create conditions for and support the successful implementation of reforms.**
- **Ensure communication about the benefits of reform and the costs of inaction.**
- **Implement the full package of policy proposals.**

📖 *Tertiary Education for the Knowledge Society: Volume 2,* 2008, Chapter 11

Among the principles and pointers for quality assurance in tertiary education, in addition to the general requisites of building the focus on student outcomes and the capacity for quality assurance are:

- **Ensure that quality assurance serves both improvement and accountability purposes,** and more generally make sure it is consistent with the goals of tertiary education.
- **Combine internal and external mechanisms** for quality assurance.
- **Make stakeholders visible in the evaluation procedures** – students, graduates and employers.
- **Enhance the international comparability** of the quality assurance framework.

📖 *Tertiary Education for the Knowledge Society: Volume 1,* 2008, Chapter 5

Among the main principles guiding funding strategies in tertiary education, beyond ensuring that they promote the wider goals and societal benefit, are:

- **Use cost-sharing between the state and students as the principle to shape the sector's funding:** There is need for public subsidies to tertiary education regardless of the sector of provision, but also for charging tuition fees to students, especially if limited public funds would ration student numbers, jeopardise spending levels per student, or restrict financial support for the disadvantaged.
- **Make institutional funding to teaching formula-driven:** The criteria for the distribution of funds to institutions need to be clear, using transparent formulae which shield allocation decisions from political pressures, while tailoring incentives to shape institutional plans towards national goals.

- **Improve cost-effectiveness:** Inefficiencies should be addressed through such means as: linking funding more closely to graduation rates, reducing public subsidies for those who stay too long in their studies; eliminating some duplicated programmes; rationalising low- or declining-enrolment programmes; increasing the use of shared facilities; and expanding student mobility across institutions.

- **Back the overall funding approach with a comprehensive student support system:** A mixed system of grants and loans assists students in covering tuition and living costs, alleviating excessive hours in paid work or disproportionate reliance on family support. In many countries student support needs to be expanded and diversified.

📖 *Tertiary Education for the Knowledge Society: Volume 1*, 2008, Chapter 4

The OECD in close cooperation with UNESCO published a set of international *Guidelines for Quality Provision in Cross-border Higher Education* in 2005 recommending actions for different stakeholders. For governments, it is recommended that they:

- Establish or encourage the establishment of a **comprehensive, fair and transparent system of registration or licensing** for cross-border higher education providers wishing to operate in their territory.

- Establish or encourage the establishment of **a comprehensive capacity for reliable quality assurance and accreditation** of cross-border higher education provision.

- **Consult and co-ordinate amongst the various competent bodies for quality assurance and accreditation,** both nationally and internationally.

- Provide accurate, reliable and easily accessible **information on the criteria and standards for registration, licensure, quality assurance and accreditation** of cross-border higher education, their consequences on the funding of students, institutions or programmes where applicable, and their voluntary or mandatory nature.

- Consider becoming party to, and contribute to, the development and/or updating of the appropriate **UNESCO regional conventions on recognition of qualifications**, and establish national information centres as stipulated by the conventions.

- Where appropriate develop or encourage **bilateral or multilateral recognition agreements**, facilitating the recognition or equivalence of each country's qualifications based on the procedures and criteria included in mutual agreements.

- Contribute to efforts to improve the accessibility at the international level of up-to-date, accurate and comprehensive **information on recognised higher education institutions/ providers.**

Recognising partial outcomes and non-formal and informal learning are ways for tertiary education to improve efficiency and equity: A considerable number of students prematurely abandon their studies or do not complete the courses they began. Recognition

of accumulated learning outcomes is one way of rationalising post-secondary education and making it less expensive. Many countries or regions use the recognition of non-formal and informal learning outcomes to grant course exemptions for those returning to tertiary education which may be extended to those who changed their course prior to its completion. Recognition of non-formal and informal learning outcomes can broaden the group of potential entrants and help to offset the decrease in enrolments among traditional students arriving from schooling.

📖 *Recognising Non-Formal and Informal Learning: Outcomes, Policies and Practices,* 2010, Chapter 3

Government has a key role to play in joining up a wide range of policies and in creating supportive environments to promote the regional role of higher education institutions. These include to:

- **Create more "joined up" decision making** (finance, education, science and technology, and industry ministries, etc.) to co-ordinate decisions on priorities and strategies in regional development.

- **Make regional engagement and its agenda for economic, social and cultural development explicit in** higher education legislation and mission strategies.

- **Develop indicators and monitor outcomes** to assess the impact of higher education institutions on regional performance, and encourage their participation in regional governance structures.

- **Provide a supportive regulatory, tax and accountability environment** for university-enterprise co-operation: what is now active regional engagement in particularly forward-looking and entrepreneurial institutions should become more widespread across the sector.

📖 *Higher Education and Regions: Globally Competitive, Locally Engaged,* 2007, Chapter 9

Beyond safeguarding high-quality pathway opportunities to tertiary education, countries need to improve transition to work opportunities: Access to tertiary education does not necessarily lead to employment. Optimising the transition to employment presupposes that the vocational education and training initiatives undertaken at secondary level to improve the employability of disabled young adults offer a real educational alternative. Tertiary education institutions need to attach the same importance to the professional future of students with disabilities as they do for other students, and they should create sufficiently deep-rooted and formalised links with the economic sphere. Active employment policies should encourage firms to recruit workers with disabilities, while admissions and support services for students with disabilities should give greater attention to access to employment and work closely with agencies that assist with job searches or find jobs for persons with disabilities.

📖 *Inclusion of Students with Disabilities in Tertiary Education and Employment,* 2011, Chapters 1-5

A recent study on institution-wide quality teaching policies of higher education institutions has identified a number of routes and levers for improving the quality of teaching.

- **Raise awareness of quality teaching:** Institutions play the key role in fostering quality teaching as national regulations rarely require or prompt academics to be trained in pedagogy or to upgrade their educational competences over their professional lives.

- **Develop excellent teachers:** This requires well-designed professional development for individual teachers, but also deans, heads of programmes and other team leaders who are drivers of change. There needs to be a collaborative reflection on the quality of teaching and learning that is aligned with university values, identity and faculty expectations.

- **Engage students:** Students have enormous capacity to leverage quality provided they are given the right tools and clarity about the objectives of their engagement. Student engagement is most powerful as a driver of quality teaching when it involves dialogue, and not only information on the student's experience.

- **Build organisations for change and teaching leadership:** Institutions are complex adaptive systems with no single pathway to achieve real teaching quality improvements. Many in an institution can be change agents provided they understand the change process and are committed to raising teaching quality. Effective leadership is crucial to quality improvement and shaping the institution's quality culture.

- **Align institutional policies to foster quality teaching:** Improvements in teaching quality can be achieved more rapidly and cost-effectively if approached collectively, underpinned by well-aligned institutional policies. Five areas stand out for institutional alignment to support policy teaching: human resources; information and computing technology; learning environments; student support; and internationalisation.

📖 *Fostering Quality Teaching in Higher Education: Policies and Practices: An IMHE Guide for higher education institutions,* 2012

References and Further Reading

Marginson, S. (2009), "The Knowledge Economy and Higher Education: A System for Regulating the Value of Knowledge", *Higher Education and Policy: Journal of the Programme on Institutional Management in Higher Education*, Vol. 21, No. 1, OECD Publishing.

OECD (2007), *Higher Education and Regions: Globally Competitive, Locally Engaged*, OECD Publishing.

OECD (2008), *Higher Education to 2030, Volume 1, Demography*, OECD Publishing.

OECD (2008), *Tertiary Education for the Knowledge Society: Volume 1*, OECD Publishing

OECD (2008), *Tertiary Education for the Knowledge Society: Volume 2*, OECD Publishing.

OECD (2009), *Higher Education to 2030, Volume 2, Globalisation*, Educational Research and Innovation, OECD Publishing.

OECD (2011), *Inclusion of Students with Disabilities in Tertiary Education and Employment*, Education and Training Policy, OECD Publishing.

OECD (2012), "How Is the Global Talent Pool Changing?", *Education Indicators in Focus*, No. 5, OECD Publishing.

OECD (2012), "What Are the Returns on Higher Education for Individuals and Countries?", Education Indicators in Focus, No. 6, OECD Publishing.

OECD (2012), *Education at a Glance 2012: OECD Indicators*, OECD Publishing.

OECD (2012), *Fostering Quality Teaching in Higher Education: Policies and Practices: An IMHE Guide for Higher Education Institutions*, OECD Publishing.

OECD (2012), *IMHE Focus: Approaches to Internationalisation and their Implications for Strategic Management and Institutional Practice*, OECD Publishing.

Vincent-Lancrin, S. and **S. Pfotenhauer** (2012), "Guidelines for Quality Provision in Cross-Border Higher Education: Where Do We Stand?", *OECD Education Working Papers*, No. 70, OECD Publishing.

Werquin, P. (2010), *Recognising Non-Formal and Informal Learning: Outcomes, Policies and Practices*, OECD Publishing.

5

Lifelong Learning and Adults

This chapter draws on various sources to examine evidence and recommendations regarding adult education and training, and lifelong learning more widely. It brings together survey information on individuals in the adult population, education system information, enterprise data, and research findings on the ageing process. Wide differences exist between countries in which organised learning is a common adult activity and where it remains much less common. The majority of the learning undertaken relates to non-formal job-related training, and in the formal education sector there are countries where very few older adults are found. Studies of ageing show the clear benefits of continued learning. Findings and conclusions from OECD studies on key areas such as financing (especially co-financing), guidance, the recognition of non-formal learning, and qualifications systems are presented, some of these from the mid-2000s. Certain education systems are more successful than others at teaching non-native languages to adults. Analysis on the literacy and life skills of adults informs the OECD Survey of Adult Skills (PIAAC) which will provide a powerful comparative data set on foundation skills and human capital in 2013.

INTRODUCTION

With agreement on the importance of lifelong learning in the OECD and by countries, it is natural that adult participation in education and training has been a focus of statistical work, research and policy analysis. The international data show how wide the variations between countries are in terms of adult participation in formal and non-formal education, with very marked differences according to the qualification levels of the adults, and also by age (see also Chapter 7). Lifelong learning has been a defining goal for education and training policies for many years, emphasising the need for organised learning to take place over the whole lifespan and across the different main spheres that make up our lives ("life-wide"). While the OECD acknowledges its importance, lifelong learning has not been the focus of holistic analyses in recent years.

The OECD has conducted international reviews bringing together the education and employment perspectives on provision and policies for adult learning, with complementary studies on qualifications, financing and the recognition of non-formal and informal learning.

Languages in a Global World, published in 2012, explores why some people are successful in learning non-native languages and others not, and why certain education systems appear more successful than others at teaching non-native languages. OECD analysis on the Adult Literacy and Lifeskills Survey has offered an overview of the foundation skills of adults in the domains prose literacy, document literacy, numeracy, problem solving and, indirectly, familiarity with and use of information and communication technologies (ICT). This work informs the ambitious OECD Survey of Adult Skills (PIAAC) which is underway and aims to publish a powerful comparative data set on foundation skills and human capital in 2013. With information from 5 000 participants in each country, it covers: key cognitive skills; educational attainment and skill formation; skill use in the workplace and elsewhere; labour market outcomes; characteristics of individuals; and changes in literacy and numeracy skills over time.

KEY FINDINGS

Only a minority of adults engage in organised formal or non-formal learning over the course of a year: Combining formal and non-formal education and training, only a minority of adults participate in such activity over a year across OECD countries as a whole (40%), even when "education" is widely understood to include short seminars, lectures or workshops. The proportion ranges widely however, from more than 60% in New Zealand and Sweden to less than 15% in Greece and Hungary. As these are overall averages, they hide still wider variations between adults of different ages or levels of education. Across OECD countries, half of 25-34 year-olds participate in formal and/or non-formal education while only about a quarter do so among 55-64 year-olds (27%). This means that there is a very wide gap between the 14% participation rate for those in the older cohort with a low level of education and a rate more than four times greater at 65% for younger adults with tertiary-level education.

📖 *Education at a Glance 2012: OECD Indicators*, 2012, Indicator C6

Only one in sixteen adults aged 30-39 is enrolled either full- or part-time in formal education in OECD countries, and students make up no more than one in 1.5% of the 40+ age group: The 20-29 year-olds enrolled in education, while all are "adults", include many who are completing their initial cycles of education and training. For older adults, 6.1% of the 30-39 year-olds across OECD countries are enrolled in education, full- or part-time. It is significantly higher than this in certain countries at 10% or more: Australia (12.0%), Finland (15.4%), Iceland (13.6%), New Zealand (11.8%) and Sweden (13.7%). Some countries are unable to make the corresponding calculations for the 40+ age group, but where they can, the highest levels of enrolment are found in Australia (4.7%), Belgium (3.7%), Finland (3.6%), Iceland (3.7%) and New Zealand (4.7%).

📖 *Education at a Glance 2012: OECD Indicators,* 2012, Indicator C1

Figure 5.1.
Participation in non-formal education, by age group (2007)

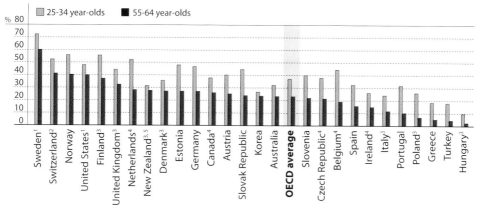

1. Year of reference 2005.
2. Year of reference 2009.
3. Year of reference 2006.
4. Year of reference 2008.
5. Excludes adults who participated only in "short seminars, lectures, workshops or special talks".
Countries are ranked in descending order of the participation rate of 55-64 year-olds (2007).
Source: OECD (2012), *Education at a Glance 2012: OECD Indicators,* OECD Publishing. Table C6.4a. See Annex 3 for notes (*www.oecd.org/edu/eag2012*).

StatLink ᔕᔕᔕ http://dx.doi.org/10.1787/888932663416

There are countries where to be enrolled in formal education as an older adult remains a very rare occurrence: With an OECD average of just above 6% for adults in their thirties in formal education, there are naturally countries where the level is significantly lower. Those at half the average enrolment rate for 30-39 year-olds or less include: France (2.7%), Germany (3%), Greece (1.0%), Korea (2.0%), Luxembourg (1.5%) and the Netherlands (3.0%).

Lack of data prevent a number of OECD countries from making the corresponding calculations for the 40+ age group; where they can do so, 0.5% or fewer of these mature adults are in full- or part-time education in the Czech Republic (0.5%), Germany (0.2%), Italy (0.1%), Korea (0.5%), Luxembourg (0.2%), Switzerland (0.5%) and Turkey (0.4%).

📖 *Education at a Glance 2012: OECD Indicators,* 2012, Indicator C1

About a third of adults across OECD countries participates in non-formal education: In 2007, on average across OECD countries, 34% of adults (25-64 year-olds) participated in non-formal education. Participation rates vary from over 50% in Finland, Norway and Sweden, at one end of the spectrum, to less than 15% in Greece, Hungary and Turkey. Young adults (25-34 year-olds) are 1.6 times more likely to participate in non-formal education than the 55-64 year-olds.

📖 *Education at a Glance 2012: OECD Indicators,* 2012, Indicator C6

Across the OECD, just over a quarter of working-age adults have recently participated in job-related learning, with the highest levels in some Nordic countries: A comfortable majority of the participants in adult educational activities are found in work-related learning. In 2007, just over a quarter of the population aged 25-64 (29%) in OECD countries participated in job-related non-formal education. The country variations are wide. The countries that register the highest participation at over 40% are Finland (44%), Norway (47%) and Sweden (61%), Switzerland (42%), with Germany and the Slovak Republic not far behind at 38%. However, less than 15% of adults participated in job-related learning in Greece (11%), Hungary (6%), Italy (14%), Korea (11%), Turkey (9%) with Poland and Portugal also under 20%. As expected, participation in such forms of learning is significantly higher among those in employment than for the unemployed across OECD countries as a whole.

📖 *Education at a Glance 2012: OECD Indicators,* 2012, Indicator C6

In the majority of OECD countries, employers invest more in the non-formal education of an employee with a high level of education than in an employee with a low level of education: In 2007, the annual cost of the working time devoted to employer-sponsored non-formal education per employee amounted to USD 931. This represents 2.4% of the average annual labour cost of an employee. The cost increases from USD 659 for employees with a low level of educational attainment to USD 1 235 for employees with high levels of education. Exceptions are Canada and Denmark, where relatively more investment goes to employees with a low level of education. The differences in investment according to the educational level of the employees are small in Estonia, Finland, the Netherlands, Norway and Sweden.

📖 *Education at a Glance 2012: OECD Indicators,* 2012, Indicator C6

Despite the common emphasis on constructing knowledge-based economies, there has been a slight downward trend in Europe in jobs using high levels of learning, discretion and complexity: Data from the European Survey of Working Conditions show that while a large share of European workers have access to work settings that call for learning and problem solving, there has been a slight downward trend over the decade from 1995 in the proportion of employees having access to work settings characterised by high levels of learning, complexity and discretion. There are important variations in the spread of learning organisations across the European Union, ranging from 65% of salaried employees in such organisations in Sweden in 2005 to only around 20% in Spain among OECD countries.

📖 *Innovative Workplaces: Learning Organisations and Innovation,* 2010, Chapter 6

Insufficient opportunities for education are not the principal reason why many adults do not engage in learning: Evidence on barriers to participation suggests that under-investment in adult learning is due more to the demand side than to lack of supply of learning opportunities. Many adults are simply not interested. This can be because they are not aware of the need for training or because of lack of information, lack of incentives or a perceived lack of returns. When asked about the obstacles, most refer to the key problem of lack of time, mainly due to work or family obligations (the opportunity costs). Lack of resources to pay for training is another issue. The time required for training and the resulting opportunity costs could be reduced through more systematic recognition of acquired skills and competences, more efficient forms of training, individualised programmes of study, and more effective information and advice. Co-financing can help to share the time costs for training as well as the direct costs.

📖 *Promoting Adult Learning,* 2005, Chapter 5

Brain research provides important additional support for adults' continued learning throughout the lifespan: One of the most powerful set of neurological findings on learning concerns the brain's remarkable properties of "plasticity" – to grow in response to experience and to prune itself when parts become unnecessary. This continues throughout the lifespan, and far further into old age than had previously been understood. The demands made on the individual and in his/her learning are key to the plasticity – the more one learns, the more one can learn. Neuroscience has shown that learning is a lifelong activity in which the more that it continues, the more effective it is.

📖 *Understanding the Brain: The Birth of a Learning Science,* 2007, Chapter 2

Brain research confirms the wider benefits of learning, especially for ageing populations: For older people, cognitive engagement, regular physical exercise and an active social life promote learning and can delay degeneration of the ageing brain. The enormous and costly problems represented by dementia in ever-ageing populations can be addressed through the learning interventions being identified through neuroscience. Combinations of improved diagnostics, opportunities to exercise, appropriate and validated pharmacological treatment, and good educational intervention can do much to maintain positive well-being and to prevent deterioration.

📖 *Understanding the Brain: The Birth of a Learning Science, 2007, Chapter 2;* "Ageing and Skills: A Review and Analysis of Skill Gain and Skill Loss Over the Lifespan and Over Time", *OECD Education Working Papers,* No. 72, 2012

Box 5.1. **Participation in adult learning for 65-74 year-olds**

In an ageing society, individuals increasingly need to stay in employment well into their sixties or seventies. Using, updating and acquiring skills remains important into retirement age as a means to promote active citizenship and social participation beyond the workplace.

In 2007, the participation of 65-74 year-olds in formal and/or non-formal learning ranged from more than 20% in the United Kingdom and the United States to 4% in Spain. In the six countries for which data are available, older women participate more often in formal and/or non-formal education than men of the same age. The steady decline in the participation rate observed for the younger age groups continues for the 55-64 year-olds although not at the same rate for all countries. In the United Kingdom and the United States, the age groups differ least in their participation rates and the participation rate of 55-64 year-olds is relatively high. The drop in participation rates from one age group to the next is largest in countries where the participation rate of the younger elderly is low, as in Spain and Ireland.

Percentage of 55-64 year-olds and 65-74 year-olds who have participated in formal and/or non-formal education, by educational attainment (2007)

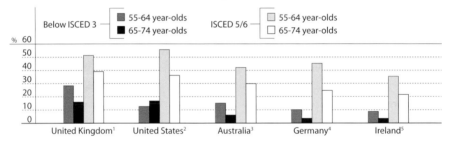

1. Year of reference 2006.
2. Year of reference 2005.
3. The data for 55-64 year-olds and 65-74 year-olds are from different survey sources.
4. Year of reference 2007.
5. Year of reference 2008.
Countries are ranked in descending order of the participation rate of 65-74 year-olds with tertiary education.
Source: OECD (2012), *Education at a Glance 2012: OECD Indicators*, OECD Publishing. Table C6.11. See Annex 3 for notes (*www.oecd.org/edu/eag2012*).

StatLink ━━ http://dx.doi.org/10.1787/888932663492

In all six countries, older persons with tertiary education participate in formal and/or non-formal education more often than those with low levels of education. In Australia, Germany, Ireland and the United Kingdom, the relative advantage of people with tertiary education is higher for the oldest age group than for the next youngest age group. The impact of educational attainment on participation rates is weaker for the young elderly in Spain and the United States.

Large proportions of adults in OECD countries and other advanced economies have low levels of proficiency in key foundation skills: OECD analysis on foundation skills, i.e. skills in prose literacy, document literacy, numeracy, problem solving, and familiarity with ICT, of adults in 11 countries or regions showed that large proportions of adults have low levels of proficiency in these key foundation skills. Significant proportions of adults display poor levels of proficiency in one or more of the skill domains and many perform poorly in all domains. Even in the best performing countries (the Netherlands and Norway), low performance in at least one skill domain is the reality for over half of the adult population. Much of the differences in the level and distribution of proficiency can be explained by social background, educational attainment and a range of variables relating to use of and engagement with literacy and numeracy and the ways adults lead their lives.

📖 *Literacy for Life: Further Results From the Adult Literacy and Lifeskills Survey,* 2011, Conclusions

There are individual and social benefits from learning non-native languages: Both individuals and societies enhance their economic prospects through the mastery of languages, so that there are personal, academic and global reasons for ensuring that students learn different languages. Research supports the spillover benefits to other academic skills from learning to speak other languages. Learning non-native languages creates appreciation for cultural differences, associated with greater tolerance.

📖 *Languages in a Global World: Learning for Better Cultural Understanding,* 2012, Executive Summary

POLICY DIRECTIONS

Developing and co-ordinating system-level policies for effective adult learning, especially engaging at-risk groups, means:

- **Developing adult learners at young ages:** This means considering as an entire portfolio the range of interventions to combat low adult attainment (training programmes, school-based policies and earlier interventions). It means reducing the rate of dropout at school level and getting those young adults who do drop out of school back into second-chance opportunities as early as possible.

- **Working towards compatibility between training and employment:** In many countries, labour market programmes and the education system are independent, with few links to permit the training involved to count towards conventional qualifications. Linking the two can facilitate the move not just into work, but into more solid careers.

- **Linking adult learning to social welfare programmes:** This is an integral aspect of active programmes – to shift away from passive welfare transfers towards training alternatives which strengthen labour market prospects. The linking of adult learning and welfare benefits policies is part of this trend.

- **Collaborating with the social partners:** Admitting the social partners into decision-making processes contributes to plans and policies concerning delivery methods, and to the recognition and certification of learning. They are key to qualification systems and may be involved in actual delivery.

📖 *Promoting Adult Learning,* 2005, Chapter 5

Co-financing is an underpinning principle for adult learners: There is considerable evidence that adult learning benefits adults themselves as well as employers and society. There are different co-financing savings and loan schemes seeking to mirror the way that benefits are shared and to leverage individual contributions with matching contributions provided by the public authorities through individual grants or tax incentives, non-governmental organisations and/or employers. Their success depends on a number of conditions:

- **The creation of new institutional structures for co-financing and a "whole of government"** approach to ensure that public authorities provide more systemic support for financing.

- **Financing schemes need to empower individual learners to choose** what, how, where and when to learn, and where to go with their acquired skills and competences.

- **Government should concentrate its resources on those individuals least able to pay** in times of scarce resources and as the benefits of lifelong learning are widely shared.

- **Co-ordinated policy making** by public authorities and their collaboration with financial institutions, social partners and other stakeholders are required in the implementation of co-financing strategies.

📖 *Co-financing Lifelong Learning: Towards a Systemic Approach,* 2004, Chapters 2 and 3

Exploit the pivotal role of qualifications systems so as to promote dynamic lifelong education and training systems: Certain aspects of qualification systems should receive attention in their implications for lifelong learning implementation, including:

- **Increase flexibility and responsiveness:** Qualifications systems responsive to the changing needs of the economy, employment and the personal ambitions of individuals are "customised", with flexibility promoted by the various mechanisms that increase choice.

- **Facilitate open access to qualifications:** Lifelong learning allows individuals to gain qualifications from different starting points, including the development of new routes to existing qualifications and calling for effective information and guidance systems.

- **Diversify assessment procedures:** Assessment methods and approaches have an important influence on the willingness of individuals to embark on a qualification; credit transfer and outcomes-based methods call for different modes of assessment.

- **Make qualifications progressive:** Accumulating learning experiences and developing competences throughout life represent a significant shift from "once and for all" initial education and training, and call for coherence in the qualifications system.

📖 *Qualifications Systems: Bridges to Lifelong Learning*, 2007, Chapter 2

The OECD has identified seven interrelated areas where policy can do more to help strengthen and develop effective practice, and improve outcomes for adults who need education to address foundation skills in language, literacy and numeracy (LLN):

- **Promote active debate on the nature of teaching, learning and assessment:** Countries need open discussion about such questions as what should be the underlying principles driving provision in the adult LLN system, and what counts as success and for whom?

- **Strengthen professionalism:** Effective teaching, learning and assessment hinge on the quality of interactions between and among educators and learners; countries will need to continue to strengthen practice through rigorous qualification and professional development requirements.

- **Balance the structure and flexibility of programmes – formative assessment as a framework:** Policies should include the development of broadly-defined learning objectives, tools for community-based and work-based programmes, guidelines on the process and the principles of formative assessment, as well as appropriate professional development.

- **Strengthen learner-centred approaches:** To ensure that learners' needs are diagnosed and addressed, individual motivations, interests and goals are incorporated into teaching, and learners may choose whether or not to pursue qualifications.

- **Diversify and deepen approaches to programme evaluation for accountability:** Given the range of stakeholder interests, no single approach can satisfy all needs. Systems that use diverse, well-aligned measures of learning processes, as well as outcomes, will be better able to manage competing goals and interests, and to capture useful data.

- **Devote the necessary resources of people, time and money:** The fragile funding and voluntary nature of much LLN provision often impedes the goals of professionalising the field and improving outcomes.

- **Strengthen the knowledge base:** There is a very large research agenda as the knowledge base remains seriously under-developed; this should include evaluations of promising teaching and assessment practices, policies and implementation, and it will need to pay much greater attention to impact.

📖 *Teaching, Learning and Assessment for Adults: Improving Foundation Skills*, 2008, Chapter 11

References and Further Reading

Della Chiesa, B., J. Scott and **C. Hinton (eds.)** (2012), *Languages in a Global World: Learning for Better Cultural Understanding,* Educational Research and Innovation, OECD Publishing.

Desjardins, R. and **A. Warnke** (2012), "Ageing and Skills: A Review and Analysis of Skill Gain and Skill Loss Over the Lifespan and Over Time", *OECD Education Working Papers,* No. 72, OECD Publishing.

OECD (2004), *Co-financing Lifelong Learning: Towards a Systemic Approach,* OECD Publishing.

OECD (2005), *Promoting Adult Learning,* OECD Publishing.

OECD (2007), *Understanding the Brain: The Birth of a Learning Science,* OECD Publishing.

OECD (2007), *Qualifications Systems: Bridges to Lifelong Learning,* OECD Publishing.

OECD (2008), *Teaching, Learning and Assessment for Adults: Improving Foundation Skills* (edited by Janet Looney), OECD Publishing.

Werquin (2010), *Recognising Non-formal and Informal Learning: Outcomes, Polices and Practices,* OECD Publishing.

OECD (2010), *Innovative Workplaces: Learning Organisations and Innovation,* OECD Publishing.

OECD (2011), *Literacy for Life: Further Results From the Adult Literacy and Lifeskills Survey,* OECD Publishing.

OECD (2012), *Education at a Glance 2012: OECD Indicators,* OECD Publishing.

Outcomes, Benefits and Returns

Very rich information on educational outcomes has been generated through OECD work, especially with the triennial Programme for International Student Assessment (PISA), which surveys the achievements of 15-year-olds in reading, mathematics, science and related aspects of competence, together with a range of associated background information. The Strong Performers and Successful Reformers in Education *series has allowed for deeper understanding of the policy trajectories and practices of those education systems that are among the "top" performers on PISA. Education is also closely related to employment outcomes and earnings, with key OECD findings reported in this chapter. Additionally there is an expanding analysis of returns to education within the OECD, with findings confirming the positive returns to higher levels of educational attainment on a variety of measures, certainly for the individual, but also for the economy at large. There are also positive returns to early childhood education and care, and to vocational education. Work on the social outcomes of education examines how education influences health, civic participation and social engagement, as well as the economic outcomes.*

The statistical data for Israel are supplied by and under the responsibility of the relevant Israeli authorities. The use of such data by the OECD is without prejudice to the status of the Golan Heights, East Jerusalem and Israeli settlements in the West Bank under the terms of international law.

INTRODUCTION

Very rich information on educational outcomes has been generated through OECD work, especially with the triennial Programme for International Student Assessment (PISA) surveys. These survey the achievement of 15-year-olds in different competence areas, together with a growing range of associated background information, and in many non-member countries and economies, as well as those of the OECD. In charting patterns, large numbers do not attain levels that might be regarded as the minimum for 21st century knowledge economies. There is also expanding analysis of returns to education within the OECD. Findings confirm the positive returns to higher levels of educational attainment on a variety of measures, certainly for the individual, but also for the economy at large. Education affects employment and earnings, but it also has an impact on an individual's well-being and contribution to society. Work on the Social Outcomes of Learning examines the evidence on how education influences health, civic participation and social engagement.

In 2010 the OECD embarked on *Strong Performers and Successful Reformers in Education* to gain deeper understanding of the policy trajectories and practices of those education systems that are among the "top" performers on PISA. The analysis has allowed for more country specific, as well as generally applicable, policy lessons.

The strong OECD focus on outcomes is expanding beyond teenage achievements as surveys of adult competences (OECD Survey of Adult Skills [PIAAC], see Chapter 5) and outcomes from higher education (Assessment of Higher Education Learning Outcomes [AHELO], see Chapter 4) are in development.

KEY FINDINGS

Among OECD countries, students in Finland and Korea are the top performers in reading literacy but Shanghai-China heads even these: Korea and Finland are the highest performing OECD countries in reading literacy in PISA 2009, with mean scores of 539 and 536 points respectively compared with the OECD average of 493. However, the partner economy Shanghai-China outperforms both of them with a mean score of 556. Across all OECD countries, 8% attained the top 5 and 6 levels; Shanghai-China had more than double this percentage (19%). Other countries with 12% or more at Level 5 or 6 were Australia, Canada, Finland, Japan, Korea, New Zealand, and the partner economies Singapore and Hong Kong-China. All these cases show significant pools of young people with the high-level literacy skills to advance social development and the knowledge economy.

📖 *PISA 2009 Result: What Students Know and Can Do: Student Performance in Reading, Mathematics and Science,* 2010, Chapter 2

Very few countries do not escape having significant minorities of students with very low performance in reading literacy: With the exception of Finland and Korea, all OECD countries have at least 10% of students who achieve at only PISA level 1 or below in reading literacy.

Figure 6.1.

How proficient are students in reading? (2009)

Percentage of students at the different levels of reading proficiency

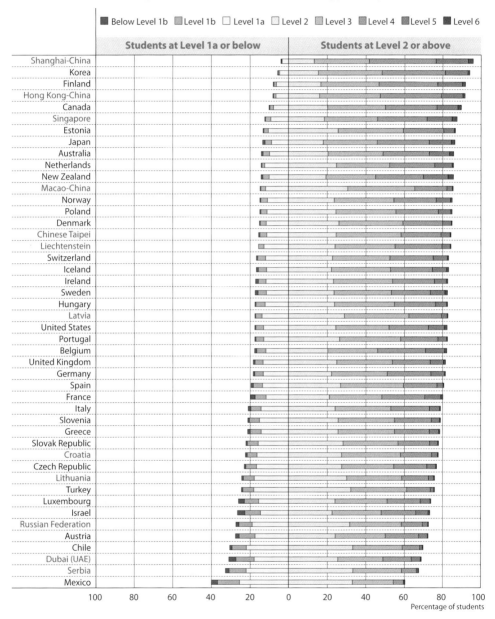

Countries are ranked in descending order of the percentage of students at Levels 2, 3, 4, 5 and 6.

Source: OECD, *PISA 2009 Database*, Table I.2.1.

StatLink ᕫᕬ᎙ http://dx.doi.org/10.1787/888932343133

In 11 OECD countries (Austria, Chile, the Czech Republic, Greece, Israel, Italy, Luxembourg, Mexico, the Slovak Republic, Slovenia and Turkey) this accounts for a fifth or more of the students. The lowest-achieving students in reading literacy make up close to third or more of 15-year-olds in Chile (31%) and Mexico (40%). The average for OECD countries is nearly one student in five not reaching Level 2, which is widely recognised as an important minimum threshold of competence for the 21st century.

📖 *PISA 2009 Result: What Students Know and Can Do: Student Performance in Reading, Mathematics and Science,* 2010, Chapter 2

Fewer than half of young people reach or surpass PISA level 3 in reading literacy – the level which involves comprehension and interpretation of moderately complex text: Across OECD countries, the majority (57%) of 15-year-old students are proficient at Level 3 or higher. For half of this 57% of the total, this is the highest level reached, making Level 3 the most common level of performance for students across OECD countries. In four countries and economies – Finland, Hong Kong-China, Korea and Shanghai-China– over three-quarters of the students are proficient at least to Level 3. On the other hand, this degree of proficiency is demonstrated by fewer than half of the students in the OECD countries Austria, Chile, the Czech Republic, Luxembourg, Mexico and Turkey.

📖 *PISA 2009 Result: What Students Know and Can Do: Student Performance in Reading, Mathematics and Science,* 2010, Chapter 2

Figure 6.2.
How proficient are students in digital reading? (2009)

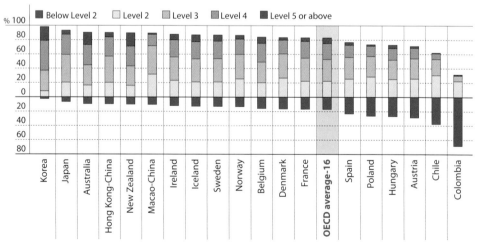

Note : "OECD average 16" includes the 16 OECD member countries appearing in this figure.
Countries are ranked in descending order of the percentage of students at Levels 2, 3, 4, 5 or above.
Source: OECD, *PISA 2009 Database,* Table VI.2.1.

StatLink ᵐˢᵖ http://dx.doi.org/10.1787/888932435378

All OECD countries, except Korea, have significant numbers of low-performing students in digital reading: In PISA 2009, all participating countries and partner economies have significant numbers of low-performing students in digital reading, with the exception of Korea. In Chile, Austria, Hungary and Poland, more than a quarter of students perform below Level 2 on digital reading, rising to as high as 70% in the partner country Colombia. Many of the students at this proficiency level can scroll and navigate across web pages, as long as explicit directions are provided, and can locate simple pieces of information in a short block of hypertext. But, they are still performing below the levels that allow full access to educational, employment and social opportunities in the 21st century.

📖 *PISA 2009 Results: Students On Line: Digital Technologies and Performance,* 2011, Chapter 2

Nine out of ten 15-year-olds in OECD countries have access to the Internet at home, but disparities still exist: 89% of 15-year-old students in 2009 reported access to the Internet at home as an OECD average; in Denmark, Finland, Iceland, the Netherlands, Norway, Sweden and Switzerland, and the partner economy Hong Kong-China, home Internet access levels are much nearer to 100%. In Mexico and 11 partner countries, less than 40% of students reported having Internet access at home. Socio-economically advantaged students reported higher levels of Internet access at home than disadvantaged students, with the socio-economic factor more important in countries with lower levels of Internet access overall. The gap between advantaged and disadvantaged students in home Internet access is more than 70 percentage points in Chile and Mexico.

📖 *PISA 2009 Results: Students On Line: Digital Technologies and Performance,* 2011, Chapter 5

PISA analyses of reading suggest that:

• **Parents should read their children books:** Reading books to children when they are just beginning primary school has a positive impact on children's reading performance. Reading at home benefits children because it shows them that reading is something that their parents value.

• **Parents should talk to their adolescent children about social, political and other issues:** Talking about social and political issues, or about books, films and television programmes with adolescent children is related to better reading performance at school. Children will enjoy reading more when they have parents who want to hear about what they have just read.

• **Parental involvement is associated with greater student engagement in school:** Parental involvement in their child's school is associated with greater student engagement in school, including participating in activities such as meeting with teachers or school principals or volunteer work at school.

• **Children should learn the positive attitude towards reading from their parents:** Children whose parents are more inclined to read and hold positive attitudes towards reading are better at reading than those who do not. Parental habits and attitudes towards intellectually engaging activities, and towards books and academic achievement, shape their child's attitudes towards reading, school and learning, and ultimately school performance as well.

📖 *Let's Read Them a Story! The Parent Factor in Education,* 2012, Chapters 1 to 5

Across OECD countries, about four in five students are proficient in mathematics at level 2 or higher: On average across OECD countries 78% of students reach or surpass PISA Level 2 – the level at which students begin to demonstrate the kind of skills that enable them to use mathematics in ways considered fundamental for their future development. In Finland and Korea, and in the partner countries and economies Shanghai-China, Hong Kong-China, Liechtenstein and Singapore, more than 90% of students perform at or above this threshold. In every OECD country except Chile, Mexico, Turkey, Israel and Greece, at least three-quarters of students are at Level 2 or above; in Chile and Mexico, more than half of all students are below Level 2.

📖 *PISA 2009 Result: What Students Know and Can Do: Student Performance in Reading, Mathematics and Science,* 2010, Chapter 3

The gender gap in science performance is small: For most OECD countries there are no statistically significant differences between young women and men. The largest gender differences in favour of boys are observed in the United States and Denmark, with 14 and 12 points, respectively, and in the partner countries Colombia and Liechtenstein, with 21 and 16 points respectively (the PISA average score in science is set at 501). In Canada, Chile, Luxembourg, Mexico, Spain, Switzerland and the United Kingdom, boys outperform girls in science with a difference that ranges from 5 to 9 points. On the other hand, girls outperform boys in science in Finland, Greece, Slovenia and Turkey, with a difference of 10 to 15 points, and in Poland with a difference of 6 points.

📖 *PISA 2009 Result: What Students Know and Can Do: Student Performance in Reading, Mathematics and Science,* 2010, Chapter 3

About one in six students are top performers in at least one of the subject areas of science, mathematics or reading: High-level skills are critical for innovation and for economic growth and social development. On average across OECD countries, 16.3% of 15-year-old students are top performers in at least one of the subject areas of science, mathematics or reading. However, only 4.1% are top performers in all three assessment subject areas: excellence is not simply strong performance across the board but can be found among a wide range of students in different subject areas. The percentage of students who are top performers in both mathematics and science (but not reading) is greater than the percentages who are top performers in reading and mathematics only or in reading and science only.

📖 *PISA 2009 Result: What Students Know and Can Do: Student Performance in Reading, Mathematics and Science,* 2010, Chapter 3

Around one in five students is consistently able to identify, explain and apply scientific concepts related to environmental topics: On average across OECD countries, 19% of 15-year-olds perform at the highest level of proficiency in environmental science in which students can consistently identify, explain and apply scientific knowledge related to a variety of environmental topics. They clearly and consistently demonstrate advanced thinking and reasoning in science relevant to the environment and can use this understanding to develop arguments relating to social and global environmental issues. In Canada, Finland and Japan, over a third of 15-year-olds have high levels of environmental literacy.

PISA in Focus No. 15, April 2012

Investment in early childhood education and care brings significant returns to individuals and society: Research from diverse countries suggests a common conclusion that investment in young children brings significant benefits not only for children and families, but also for society at large. High-quality early childhood services lay a strong foundation of learning which is fundamental to the rest of the lives of the individuals involved. Children from disadvantaged backgrounds, in particular, benefit from acquiring such a foundation. Early childhood investments bring: significant educational, social, economic and labour market returns; improved transitions from one educational level to the next; higher achievement; and lower crime rates among teenagers. Lack of investment in children's services can result in child-care shortages and unequal access, even segregation, of children according to income. Unavailability of services raises barriers against women's full-time employment – with the economic and social consequences which flow from that – and tends to channel women towards low-paid, part-time jobs.

Starting Strong II: Early Childhood Education and Care, 2006, Annex D

Attaining at least upper secondary education is an important hedge against the risk of unemployment: The unemployment rate among those adults aged 25-64 years with an upper secondary education is clearly lower than among those who have not got further that the lower secondary level – on average nearly 5 percentage points lower in 2010. This gap is particular high in the Czech Republic (16.6 percentage point gap), Hungary (14) and the Slovak Republic (28.6), and is also high in Estonia (9.6) and Germany (9.0), and in these countries the gap has grown over the past decade. Expressing this upper secondary advantage as a ratio of unemployment rates, those with upper secondary education are half or less than half as likely to be unemployed compared with those with lower secondary education in Austria, Belgium, the Czech Republic, Germany, Hungary, Norway and the Slovak Republic. There is a group of countries however – Chile, Greece, Korea, Mexico and Turkey – in which the unemployment risk among those finishing education at the lower level is slightly smaller, compared with the upper secondary level.

Education at a Glance 2012: OECD Indicators, 2012, Indicator A7

Figure 6.3.

Relative earnings from employment among 25-64 year-olds, by level of educational attainment and gender (2010)

Upper secondary and post-secondary non-tertiary education = 100

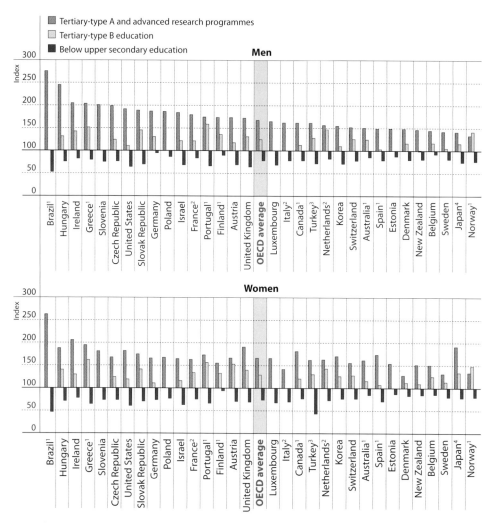

Note: Belgium, Korea and Turkey report earnings net of income tax.

1. Year of reference 2009.

2. Year of reference 2008.

3. Year of reference 2005.

4. Year of reference 2007.

Countries are ranked in descending order of the relative earnings of 25-64 year-old men with tertiary-type A education (including advanced research programmes).

Source: OECD (2012), *Education at a Glance 2012: OECD Indicators*, OECD Publishing. Table A8.1. See Annex 3 for notes (www.oecd.org/edu/eag2012).

StatLink ᴍᴤ⊓ http://dx.doi.org/10.1787/888932662143

In most countries the earnings pay-off for adults having acquired an upper secondary education is clear... but not everywhere: In 2010, the countries with the highest earnings advantage of those with upper secondary compared with lower secondary education for all working-age adults are Austria, Korea, Luxembourg, the Slovak Republic, the United Kingdom and the United States; in these countries, those with the lower attainments earn around only two-thirds to 70% of upper secondary graduates. Women who have not attained an upper secondary education are particularly disadvantaged in Greece, Israel, Italy, Luxembourg, Portugal, Turkey, The United Kingdom, the United States and partner country Brazil, where they earn less than 70% those of women with an upper secondary education. The same situation applies to men in Austria, Israel, Luxembourg, Portugal, the Slovak Republic, the United Kingdom, the United States, and partner country Brazil. There is, however, a small number of countries in which the earnings advantage of upper secondary graduates is not particularly marked – the lower attainers earn 85% or more of those with upper secondary education – as is found in Belgium and Estonia for men and women, Germany and Poland for men, and New Zealand for women.

📖 *Education at a Glance 2012: OECD Indicators,* 2012, Indicator A8

There is a strong positive relationship between education and the average earnings of individuals with tertiary-level attainments: In all countries, graduates of tertiary education earn substantially more than upper secondary graduates who in turn earn more than those whose attainment does not go beyond basic education. Earnings differentials between higher education and upper secondary graduates are generally greater than between upper and lower secondary graduates. The earnings premium for tertiary over upper secondary graduates, all adult ages and men and women combined, ranges from a high of 2.10 times the incomes of the upper secondary group in Hungary to a modest 1.24 higher in New Zealand.

📖 *Education at a Glance 2012: OECD Indicators,* 2012, Indicator A8

Even adding in the costs of acquiring more education, the higher average subsequent earnings mean that it pays to continue to upper over lower secondary education: For men and women, continuing on to upper secondary education after the lower secondary level pays off on average in all countries. For men, this "private" rate of return stands at 13.4% on average across the 25 OECD countries permitting these calculations, and over 15% in 5 of these countries. The range lies between 6.7% in Germany, to 40.8% in the Slovak Republic. The range is greater for women, lying between 4.9% in Finland, up to 42.8% in the Slovak Republic. The average individual rate of return for women for upper secondary education is 13%.

📖 *Education at a Glance 2012: OECD Indicators,* 2012, Indicator A9

Pursuing a tertiary education can entail significant costs, but the long-term economic benefits, for both individuals and countries, are sizable, too: An individual invests on average about USD 55 000 to acquire a tertiary qualification on average across the OECD countries. However, the personal benefits are sizeable, too. The returns are typically higher for men who can expect an average net gain of USD 162 000, whereas a woman can expect a net gain of USD 110 000. Although public investments in tertiary education are large in many countries so are the net public returns. They average at over USD 100 000 for men, almost three times the public investment involved. For women, the net public return is almost twice the level of public investment. In sum, the long-term economic benefits of investing in tertiary education are good for both individuals and countries, and will probably remain so for the foreseeable future.

📖 *Education at a Glance 2012: OECD Indicators, 2012, Indicator A9;* "What Are the Returns on Higher Education for Individuals and Countries?", *Education Indicators in Focus,* No. 6, 2012

The returns to tertiary compared with upper secondary education are also positive across OECD countries: The relative advantage of continuing on to acquire tertiary over upper secondary education is also positive in all the countries with data. For men, it is 12.4% and for women 11.4% in the 28 countries permitting calculations. The rate of return advantage of continuing to tertiary beyond upper secondary rises to 20% or more for men in Hungary, Poland and the Slovak Republic, and to 19% or more for women in Poland, the Slovak Republic and Turkey. The countries where the rates of return to higher education are lower for men than women are Australia, Belgium, Canada, Denmark, Japan, Korea, Norway and Spain.

📖 *Education at a Glance 2012: OECD Indicators,* 2012, Indicator A9

Projections suggest that there are enormous economic gains to be obtained by OECD countries that can improve the cognitive skills – and not just the educational attainment – of their populations: Projections based on historical relationships (bearing in mind the uncertainties of future projections) suggest that if all OECD countries could boost their average PISA scores by 25 points over the next two decades, the aggregate gain of OECD GDP would be USD 115 trillion over the lifetime of the generation born in 2010. Even more ambitious goals, such as bringing all students to the OECD level of minimal proficiency – a PISA score of 400 – are associated with aggregate GDP increases of nearly USD 200 trillion. Bringing all countries up to the OECD's best performing education system in PISA, Finland, would result in gains in the order of USD 260 trillion. It is the quality of learning outcomes, not the length of schooling, which makes the difference.

📖 *The High Cost of Low Educational Performance: The Long-run Economic Impact of Improving PISA Outcomes,* 2010

Public investment in initial vocational education and training (VET) can make up for insufficient employer provision and delivers good economic returns: Much occupation-specific training is provided by employers but, if left to themselves, they will often not provide their own employees with sufficient training, particularly in transferable skills. Initial VET is designed to fill the gap by providing the needed skills, and research has shown that it can yield good economic returns from the public investment involved. Countries with strong initial VET systems like Germany have been relatively successful in tackling youth unemployment.

📖 *Learning for Jobs,* 2010, Chapter 1

OECD analysis on the social outcomes of learning suggests that education promotes health and civic and social engagement.

- **Education can play a significant role in promoting well-being and social progress and is a cost-effective way to do so:** Education is associated with a variety of social outcomes, such as better health, stronger civic and social engagement, and reduced crime, and is a relatively cost-effective means of improving health, including school-based interventions to tackle obesity, and reducing crime. Hence, education policy has health policy implications.

- **Education empowers individuals by increasing their knowledge and their cognitive, social and emotional skills, as well as improving attitudes towards lifestyles and active citizenship:** Education helps people make competent decisions by providing information, improving cognitive skills, and strengthening socio-emotional capabilities, such as resilience, self-efficacy and social skills.

- **Education's potential cannot be realised in isolation:** Children only spend about half of their non-sleeping hours in schools. Certain home and community environments can undermine, for instance, school-based actions to promote healthy lifestyles and habits when children have easy access to fast-food eating or when they indulge in sedentary activities at home.

- **Education's potential will be limited if children's cognitive, social and emotional skills are not developed early:** Essential competencies are better acquired even before children start compulsory schooling. Basic cognitive skills, positive attitudes, healthy habits and other personality traits such as patience, self-efficacy and self-confidence, need to be nurtured in the family environment early in life.

📖 *Improving Health and Social Cohesion through Education*, 2010, Chapter 4 to 6

Recognition of non-formal and informal learning delivers economic, educational, social and psychological benefits: Recognition of non-formal and informal learning generates economic benefits: it reduces both the costs associated with, and the time required to acquire qualifications in, formal education. It also allows human capital to be deployed more productively by giving people access to jobs that better match their true skills. Recognition provides educational benefits by helping people learn about themselves and develop their career within a lifelong learning framework. It provides social benefits by improving equity through giving access to further education and the labour market to disadvantaged minority groups, disaffected youth, and older workers who missed out on education earlier. Recognition can provide psychological benefits by making people aware of their capabilities and offering external validation of their worth.

📖 *Recognising Non-formal and Informal Learning: Outcomes, Policies and Practices*, 2010, Executive Summary

Box 6.1. **Education and life expectancy**

Education is an important predictor of life expectancy. On average, among 15 OECD countries, a 30-year-old male tertiary graduate can expect to live another 51 years, while a 30-year-old man who has not completed upper secondary education can expect to live only an additional 43 years. These differences are particularly large among men in Central European countries. On average, a 30-year-old male tertiary graduate in the Czech Republic can expect to live 17 years longer than a 30-year-old man who has not completed upper secondary education.

Difference in life expectancy by educational attainment at age 30 (2010)

Differences between those with "tertiary eduation"
and "below upper secondary education" at age 30, by gender

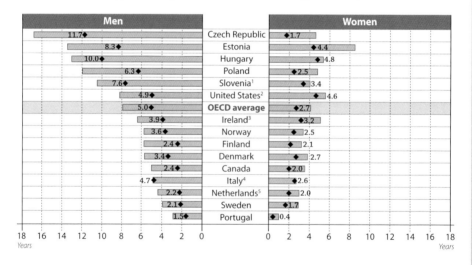

Note: The figures describe the differences in the expected years of life remaining at age 30 across education levels.
1. Year of reference 2009.
2. Year of reference 2005.
3. Year of reference 2006.
4. Year of reference 2008.
5. Year of reference 2007-10.
Countries are ranked in descending order of the difference in life expectancy among men at age 30.
Source: OECD (2012), *Education at a Glance 2012: OECD Indicators*, OECD Publishing. Table A11.1. See Annex 3 for notes (www.oecd.org/edu/eag2012).

StatLink ᐩᐩ http://dx.doi.org/10.1787/888932662390

...

There are substantial gender differences in life expectancy, and in the relationships between education and life expectancy as life expectancy differences by education are generally much smaller among women. On average among 15 OECD countries, male tertiary graduates can expect to live 8 years longer than those who have not attained upper secondary education, while a tertiary-educated woman can expect to live 4 years longer than a woman without an upper secondary education and in Portugal, only for one additional year.

Educational attainment positively enhances health, political interest and trust, with thresholds for the upper secondary level and for political interest at the tertiary level : Adults with higher levels of educational attainment are generally more likely to report that their health is at least good, that they are at least fairly interested in politics, and believe that most people can be trusted. For health, the step in attainment from lower to upper secondary education tends to show up as most influential, while the step up to tertiary is more apparent regarding political interest; no consistent thresholds are apparent regarding trust. The association between education and social outcomes generally remains strong even after adjusting for age, gender and income.

📖 *Education at a Glance 2012: OECD Indicators*, 2012, Indicator A11; *Improving Health and Social Cohesion through Education*, 2010

POLICY DIRECTIONS

OECD analysis of education systems that are among the "top performers" on PISA has allowed certain policy and governance characteristics of those systems to emerge:

- **Develop a commitment to education:** In the highest performance systems, teachers are typically paid better relative to others, education credentials are valued more, and a higher share of educational spending is devoted to instructional services.

- **Develop a conviction that all students can achieve at high levels:** Evidence shows it takes a concerted, multifaceted programme of policy making, capacity building and the development of proof points to get to the point at which most educators believe that all students can achieve high levels of performance.

- **Establish ambitious, focused and coherent education standards shared across the system and aligned with high-stakes gateways and instructional systems:** The development of world-class academic standards for students tends to be a consistent predictor of the overall performance of education systems. Such standards shape high-performing education systems by establishing rigorous, focused and coherent content at all grade levels; reducing overlap in curricula across grades and variation in implemented curricula across classrooms; facilitating co-ordination of policy drivers, ranging from curricula to teacher training; and reducing inequity in curricula across socio-economic groups.

- **Balance local responsibility with a capable centre with authority and legitimacy to act:** PISA shows the relationship between the relative autonomy of schools and schooling outcomes across systems – when autonomy is coupled with accountability. Once the state has set clear expectations for students, school autonomy in defining the details of the curriculum and assessment relates positively to the system's overall performance.

- **Ensure coherence of policies and practices:** In high performing education systems, policies and practices tend to be aligned across all aspects of the system, coherent over sustained periods of time, and consistently implemented without excessive administrative control.

- **Ensure an outwards orientation of the system to keep it evolving, and to recognise challenges and potential future threats to current success:** Strong and consistent effort to apply disciplined international benchmarking and incorporate the results of that benchmarking into policy and practice is a common characteristic of the highest-performing countries and economies.

📖 *Lessons from PISA for the United States, Strong Performers and Successful Reformers in Education,* 2011, Chapter 11

The quality of an education system depends critically on the quality of its teachers and their capacity to exercise their professional expertise. Therefore, countries should take great care in:

- **Attracting high-quality teachers:** Raising the status of the profession, the bar to enter into the profession and the recruitment of top-performing graduates are some of the policy means that have proven their potential.

- **Investing in the preparation of teachers:** teacher education programmes in the top-performing countries:

  - Are moving their initial teacher-education programmes towards a model based on preparing professionals in clinical settings, in which they get into schools earlier, spend more time there and get more and better support in the process.

  - Put more emphasis on developing the capacity to diagnose student problems swiftly and accurately.

  - Are working to develop the capacity to draw from a wide repertoire of possible solutions those that are particularly appropriate to the diagnosis.

  - Strengthen the specific instructional techniques appropriate for the subjects that the prospective teacher will teach.

  - Some countries develop research skills to enable teachers to improve their practice in a highly disciplined way.

- **Developing teacher quality once they are in the workforce:** Supervision, coaching, induction programmes, reduction of workload in initial years, allocating sufficient hours for personal development and using teacher appraisal systems to steer the personal development of teachers are among the effective policy means to support new teachers.

- **Engaging collaboratively with unions and teacher associations on quality:** There is a relationship between the degree to which teacher work has been professionalised and student performance: the higher a country on the international league tables, the more likely that it is treating its teachers as trusted professional partners and working constructively with its unions.

- **Providing a work organisation in which teachers can use their potential:** The school organisation should allow its staff both the responsibility and the authority to design, manage, budget for and organise the school's programme in its entirety, within the framework provided by the goals, curricula, examinations and qualifications systems put in place by the state.

- **Institutionalising improved practice:** High-performing countries generally consider teaching a profession in which teachers work together to frame what they believe to be good practice, conduct field-based research to confirm or disprove the approaches they develop, and then judge their colleagues by the degree to which they use proven effective practices in their classrooms. The continuous search for more effective teaching practices allows standards of practice to emerge and improvement over time.

📖 *Lessons from PISA for the United States, Strong Performers and Successful Reformers in Education,* 2011, Chapter 11

Education needs to re-invent itself in order to improve the performance of systems and to raise value for money: This will be a tremendous challenge for public policy. It will require often supply-driven education systems to develop effective mechanisms to understand and respond to rapidly-changing economic and social demands for competencies. Effective policies will require understanding not just of the development of competencies, but also of how effectively economies use their talent pool, and of how competencies in turn feed into better jobs, higher productivity, and positive economic and social outcomes. The success of education systems will be measured less by how much countries spend on education or how many complete a degree, and more by the educational outcomes achieved and by their impact on economic and social progress.

📖 *Education at a Glance 2010: OECD Indicators,* 2010, Editorial

Countries should aim to secure similar student performance among schools: Low "between-school variation" means that there is no obvious advantage in terms of performance for a student to attend one school as opposed to another – they all perform to broadly equal levels. In three countries – Norway, Finland and Iceland – less than 10% of variation in mathematics achievement in 2003 was accounted for by such differences – all the rest of the variation is "within-school". The OECD average was much higher than 10% in 2003 and stood at almost exactly a third. Securing similar student performance among schools is both important in itself as a policy goal and is compatible with high overall performance standards.

📖 *Education at a Glance 2006: OECD Indicators,* 2006, Indicator A5

Clarify returns to training by augmenting information and removing structural barriers, and by making the outcomes more transparent to individuals and firms: Effective dissemination of information can help convince individuals and firms of the benefits of training. Cost/benefit analysis provides information that can encourage and motivate adults to learn, as well as clarifying who should cover the financial costs. Efforts to stimulate firms to invest in training would be assisted by promoting the transparency of human capital investments in company accounting. Acting directly on increasing the returns to training through alternative mechanisms, such as embedding skill improvements in the wage determination process, can improve training take-up and firm productivity. National qualifications systems provide greater clarity in this respect and recognition of informal and non-formal learning contributes to reducing the opportunity cost of learning.

📖 *Promoting Adult Learning,* 2005, Chapter 2

References and Further Reading

OECD (2005), *Promoting Adult Learning*, OECD Publishing.

OECD (2006), *Starting Strong II: Early Childhood Education and Care*, OECD Publishing.

OECD (2006), *Education at a Glance 2006: OECD Indicators*, OECD Publishing.

OECD (2007), *Understanding the Social Outcomes of Learning*, OECD Publishing.

OECD (2010), *The High Cost of Low Educational Performance: The Long-run Economic Impact of Improving PISA Outcomes*, OECD Publishing.

OECD (2010), *Improving Health and Social Cohesion through Education*, OECD Publishing.

OECD (2010), *Education at a Glance 2010: OECD Indicators*, OECD Publishing.

OECD (2010), *Learning for Jobs*, OECD Publishing.

OECD (2010), *PISA 2009 Result: What Students Know and Can Do: Student Performance in Reading, Mathematics and Science (Volume I)*, OECD Publishing

OECD (2010), *PISA 2009 Result: Learning to Learn: Student Engagement, Strategies and Practices (Volume III)*, OECD Publishing

OECD (2011), *Lessons from PISA for the United States:* Strong Performers and Successful Reformers in Education, OECD Publishing.

OECD (2011), *Against the Odds: Disadvantaged Students who Succeed in School*, OECD Publishing.

OECD (2011), *PISA 2009 Results: Students On Line: Digital Technologies and Performance (Volume VI)*, OECD Publishing

OECD (2012), *PISA in Focus, Issue No. 15, April 2012*, OECD Publishing

OECD (2012), *Let's Read Them a Story: The Parent Factor in Education*, OECD Publishing

OECD (2012), *Untapped Skills: Realising the Potential of Immigrant Students*, OECD Publishing

OECD (2012), "What Are the Returns on Higher Education for Individuals and Countries?", *Education Indicators in Focus*, No. 6, OECD Publishing.

OECD (2012), *Education at a Glance 2012: OECD Indicators*, OECD Publishing.

Werquin (2010), *Recognising Non-formal and Informal Learning: Outcomes, Polices and Practices*, OECD Publishing.

7

Equity and Equality of Opportunity

Analyses of developments and policies that influence equity have been an underlying priority in much of the OECD educational work. The persistent patterns of inequality have been highlighted, with the increasing quality of international data permitting analyses relating to many pertinent groups of learners and their educational experiences. The dimensions and groups include gender, age, migrant status, special needs and social background, and cover adult formal and non-formal learning, as well as schooling, vocational education and higher education. OECD analysis has also charted the nature of the "digital divide". Findings and recommendations from a major international review of equity in education that resulted in two publications – No More Failures *and* Equity and Quality and Education *– are presented. The chapter reports promising policy directions from studies, including those on immigrants' education, cultural diversity and teacher education*

The statistical data for Israel are supplied by and under the responsibility of the relevant Israeli authorities. The use of such data by the OECD is without prejudice to the status of the Golan Heights, East Jerusalem and Israeli settlements in the West Bank under the terms of international law.

INTRODUCTION

Analyses of developments and policies that influence equity have been an underlying priority in much of the OECD educational work. The persistent patterns of inequality have been highlighted, with the increasing quality of international data permitting analyses relating to many pertinent groups of learners and their educational experiences. OECD analysis has shown that there need be no contradiction between equity and efficiency, and indeed has underlined how damaging to economic as well as social goals is the phenomenon of exclusion and widespread under-achievement.

A major international review of equity in education resulted in *No More Failures,* published in 2007, which outlines ten broad policy directions around the design of provision, practices and resourcing. The second report of the review – *Equity and Quality in Education,* published in 2012 – provides five core recommendations for preventing school failure and promoting the completion of upper secondary and a further five for supporting the improvement of low-performing disadvantaged schools. The charting of the outcomes of, and opportunities and policies for, different population groups has been undertaken across the many sectors of education and training, including longstanding work on special educational needs.

Ethnic and cultural diversity makes society richer, but reaping the full benefits requires special efforts from the education system. The OECD *Thematic Reviews on Migrant Education* have examined the education outcomes of the children of immigrants in five OECD countries. *PISA 2009 Results: Overcoming Social Background* complements this work as it provides rich insight into the equity in learning opportunities and outcomes of students with different socio-economic backgrounds. Diversity in the classroom can enhance learning and prepare students for the outside world but major challenges are facing many schools and teachers to make this happen; work on "Teacher Education for Diversity" has examined how countries educate teachers to respond to increasing cultural diversity and the educational challenges faced by indigenous populations.

KEY FINDINGS

There is no contradiction between equity and efficiency in education: Equity and efficienty are complementary, in contradiction to the widespread argument that the redistribution of resources to those in greatest need helps equity but damages efficiency. The complementarity is clear within basic education where school failure has large costs not only to those involved, but also to society, because the welfare costs of social exclusion are large. Successful secondary education completion gives individuals better employment and healthier lifestyle prospects resulting in greater contributions to public budgets and investment. More educated people contribute to more democratic societies and sustainable economies, and are less dependent on public aid and less vulnerable to economic downturns. Reasonably-priced, effective measures to address failure benefit both efficiency and equity.

Some analyses even suggest that an equitable distribution of skills across populations has a strong impact on overall economic performance.

📖 *Equity and Quality in Education: Supporting Disadvantaged Students and Schools,* 2012, Chapter 1; *No More Failures: Ten Steps to Equity in Education,* 2007

Investing early enhances both equity in education and economic efficiency: Strengthening equity in education is cost-beneficial, and investing in early years yields high returns, since it makes it possible to reap the benefits and reinforce equity efforts made at subsequent education levels. Early acquisition of skills and knowledge makes it easier to acquire skills and knowledge later on. So, strengthening equity includes investing in the very early years as well as ensuring that students complete upper secondary education.

📖 *Equity and Quality in Education: Supporting Disadvantaged Students and Schools,* 2012, Chapter 1

The countries with high quality and high equity have embraced student heterogeneity and avoided premature and differentiated structures: Early tracking is associated with reduced equity in outcomes and sometimes weakens results overall. In countries with early selection of students into highly differentiated education systems, differences among schools are large and the relationship between socio-economic background and student school performance stronger.

📖 *No More Failures: Ten Steps to Equity in Education,* 2007, Chapter 3

Choice may stimulate quality but with risks for equity: There are quality arguments to be made in favour of creating a degree of choice as a vehicle for stimulating improvement. When choices exist, schools must then look beyond their own walls at what others – their potential "competitors" – are doing; without some room for exit to be exercised, parents and students have no threat to back up voice. OECD work confirms that better educated, middle-class parents are more likely to avail themselves of choice opportunities and send their children to the "best" school they can find, widening the gaps between the sought-after schools and the rest. Across countries, greater choice in school systems is associated with larger differences in the social composition of different schools.

📖 *No More Failures: Ten Steps to Equity in Education,* 2007, Chapter 3; *Demand-sensitive Schooling? Evidence and Issues,* 2006

Boys with disabilities and receiving additional resources outnumber such girls by approximately 60 to 40, and the gap is even wider for those with learning and behavioural difficulties: These are consistent results, repeatedly found in different studies with different methodologies. There is a consistent majority of males over females in special needs education provision or in receipt of additional resources for disabilities and learning difficulties. Whether looked at by location (special school, special class, regular class), cross-nationally or nationally, age of student or stage of education, boys outnumber girls. For learning difficulties, the difference is even larger with males outnumbering females by two-thirds to one-third.

📖 *Students with Disabilities, Learning Difficulties and Disadvantages: Policies, Statistics and Indicators – 2007 Edition,* 2008, Chapter 4

The digital divide defined by technology access has faded in schools but a second one based on digital competence more stubbornly remains: In almost all OECD countries, students attend schools equipped with computers and most of these are connected to the Internet (though there do remain some gaps in digital home access). A more stubborn digital divide is that between those who have the necessary competences and skills to benefit from computer use, and those who do not, which competences are closely linked to students' economic, cultural and social capital. School use of digital media can help to reduce the digital divide, and computer use is associated with improved academic skills and competences.

📖 *Are the New Millennium Learners Making the Grade? Technology Use and Educational Performance in PISA,* 2010, Chapters 4 and 5, and Executive Summary

Immigrant students largely face greater difficulties in education than their native peers: The performance of immigrant students in reading, science and mathematics in compulsory education is for the most part lower than that of their native peers. This is despite generally positive attitudes towards learning among immigrant students. In some countries immigrant students (first-generation) are less likely to attend early childhood education and care, and more likely to repeat a grade, attend vocational schools and drop out from secondary education. They have more limited access to quality education. They are more likely to attend schools that are located in big cities that serve students who are on average from less advantaged socio-economic backgrounds and with higher concentrations of other immigrant students.

📖 *Closing the Gap for Immigrant Students: Policies, Practice, and Performance,* 2010, Chapter 2; *Where Immigrant Students Succeed: A Comparative Review of Performance and Engagement in PISA 2003,* 2006, Chapter 2

Language is an obstacle to school achievement for many immigrant students: The most obvious challenge for many students with immigrant parents is adapting to a new language and a new learning environment. PISA results suggest that the older a child is at arrival, the less well he or she does in reading at age 15. However, at least as far as reading outcomes are concerned, there does not seem to a be a critical age for language learning – i.e. there is no arrival age after which there is an abrupt fall-off in performance. Not all the decline with age of arrival is related to the language barrier itself, but rather to the fact that some students have spent significant time in an education system in the origin country with different standards, curricula, and instructional characteristics. For many, immigration means not only learning a new language, but also adapting to a more demanding education system.

📖 *Untapped Skills: Realising the Potential of Immigrant Students,* 2012, Chapter 3 and Executive Summary

Young adults born abroad are much more likely than the others to be already out of education and not to have completed upper secondary education (but with notable exceptions): Many more young adults aged 20-24 years old have low educational attainment – as indicated by having already left education without having completed at the least upper secondary education – when they are born outside the country. Across the OECD, a quarter of this age group born abroad has low attainment on this measure as compared with only 15% of those born in the country. The gap is 20 percentage points or more in Austria, Greece, Italy and the United States. Yet, not everywhere do immigrant young adults lag behind the rest of the population in educational attainment: a higher proportion of foreign-born 20-24 year-olds are still in education or already have upper secondary education in Australia, Canada, Hungary, Portugal and the United Kingdom than those born in the country.

📖 *Education at a Glance 2010: OECD Indicators,* 2010, Indicator C3

Students' attainment is typically lower in schools where most of the students come from disadvantaged backgrounds: In most OECD countries, students' attainment is typically lower in schools where most of the students come from disadvantaged backgrounds. The primary reasons for this are that students' socio-economic background has a strong impact on their performance, which many disadvantaged schools are unable to counteract; indeed, they may accentuate it. Lack of systemic support and flexibility and limited or ineffective use of resources including staff, make imposing the challenges facing low-performing disadvantaged schools.

📖 *Equity and Quality in Education: Supporting Disadvantaged Students and Schools,* 2012, Chapter 3

Figure 7.1.
Prevalence of first- and second-generation immigrant students (2009)

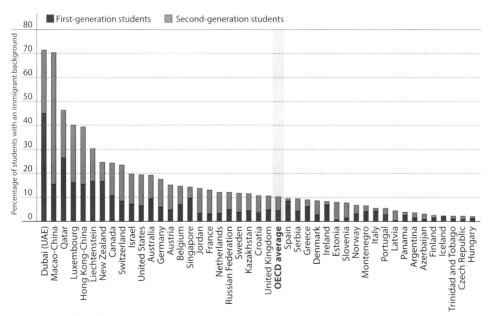

Countries are ranked in descending order of the percentage of students with an immigrant background (first- or second-generation students).
Source: OECD, *PISA 2009 Database,* Table II.4.1.

StatLink ᴀᴤᴤ http://dx.doi.org/10.1787/888932343608

High levels of immigration do not inevitably, as often assumed, lower the mean performance of school systems: In New Zealand, Canada and Switzerland, 20% to 25% of students are from an immigrant background while the proportions are even higher in Liechtenstein (30%), Hong Kong-China (39%), Luxembourg (40%) and Qatar (46%). In Macao-China and Dubai (UAE), that percentage is at least 70%. There is no positive association between the size of the immigrant student population and average performance at the country or economy level, and there is also no relationship between the proportion of students with an immigrant background and the performance gaps between native and immigrant students.

📖 *PISA Results 2009: Overcoming Social Background: Equity in Learning Opportunities and Outcomes,* 2010, Chapter 4 and Executive Summary

Figure 7.2.
Gender differences in reading performance in PISA (2009)

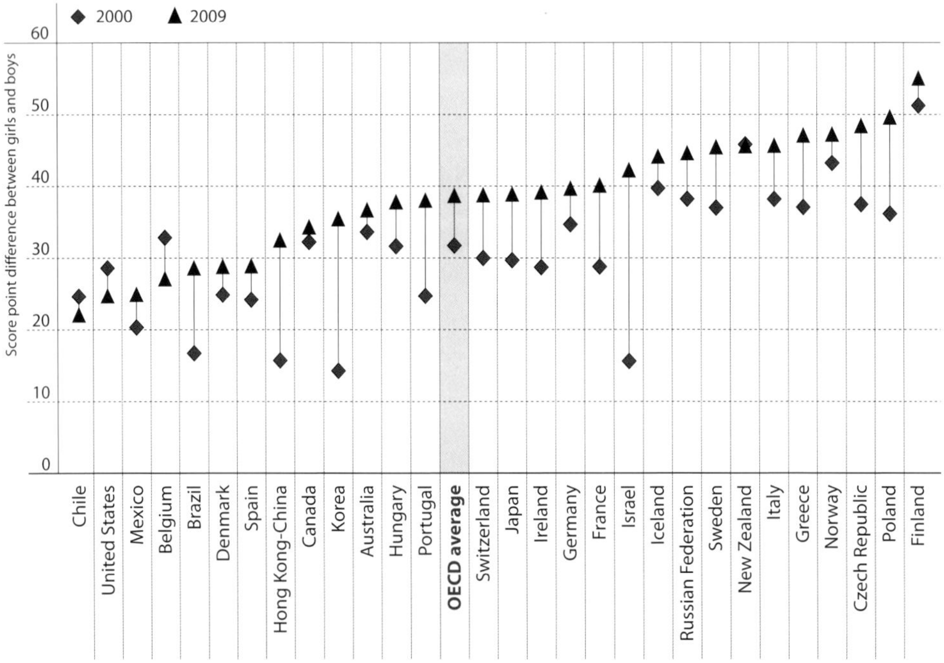

How to read this chart: The chart shows the difference in reading performance between girls and boys and the trend observed between 2000 (diamonds) and 2009 (triangles). Countries are ranked in ascending order by the difference observed in 2009. For example in Sweden, girls obtained 46 score points more in reading on average in the 2009 PISA assessment, which is roughly equivalent to one year of schooling, while in 2000 the difference amounted to only 37 score points. Non-OECD member countries and economies are included for comparison.

Source: OECD (2010), *PISA 2009 Results: Overcoming Social Background: Equity in Learning Opportunities and Outcomes (Volume II),* PISA, OECD Publishing.

StatLink 🔗 http://dx.doi.org/10.1787/888932560892

Among the 13 countries that showed clear improvements in average reading performance since 2000, most can attribute those gains to improvements among the lowest performing students: Among the 26 OECD countries with comparable results in the 2000 and 2009 PISA assessments, Chile, Germany, Hungary, Israel, Korea, Poland, Portugal, and the partner countries Albania, Brazil, Indonesia, Latvia, Liechtenstein and Peru all show overall improvements in reading performance. With the exception of Korea and Brazil, the gap in reading scores between the highest- and lowest performing students narrowed in all of these countries; and in some the impact of socio-economic background on performance weakened between 2000 and 2009. Most commonly, the reading performance of girls improved, while boys' reading performance improved in only five of the countries. While the percentage of low performers changed only slightly on average across OECD countries, it dropped from nearly half (48%) of all 15-year-old students to below one-third (31%) in Chile, from 26% to less than 18% in Portugal, and from 23% to 15% (and below the OECD average) in Poland.

📖 *PISA in Focus No. 2,* March 2011

Girls outperform boys in reading, and the gap is growing: The educational gender gap in reading performance has widened in most OECD countries since the year 2000. On average across OECD countries, 15-year-old boys are about one-and-a-half times more likely to have low reading scores than girls. The difference in score points is equivalent to one school year. Differences between boys and girls in attainment appear early on and boys are more likely to repeat school years than girls. Boys predominate among early school leavers and a higher proportion of girls receive an upper secondary school qualification. Girls usually obtain higher grades and higher pass rates in school leaving examinations, which, in turn, helps them to enter desired university programmes.

📖 *PISA Results 2009: What Students Know and Can Do: Student Performance in Reading, Mathematics and Science,* 2010, Chapter 2; *Equity and Quality in Education: Supporting Disadvantaged Students and Schools,* 2012, Chapter 1

Girls and women have now moved clearly ahead of boys and men in education: The number of expected years in formal education between ages 15 and 29 across OECD countries enjoyed by young women – 7.2 years – now surpasses those of young men who average only 6.9 and is higher in all OECD countries (2010) except Germany, Japan, Korea, Mexico, the Netherlands, Switzerland and Turkey. On average, 74% of girls complete their upper secondary education within the stipulated time, compared with 66% of boys. Only in Finland, Japan, Korea, the Slovak Republic and Sweden is there a difference of less than five percentage points in the proportions of boys and girls who leave school early. Female graduation rates from upper secondary education are higher in 24 of the 26 OECD countries permitting comparison. The female advantage is greatest in Iceland and Portugal, where graduation rates among young women exceed those of young men by 20 percentage points or more. The exception is Germany, where the graduation rate is slightly higher for young men. In entry to university-type tertiary education, only in Japan and Mexico do more men enter than women.

📖 *Education at a Glance 2012: OECD Indicators,* 2012, Indicators A2, C3 and C5

Figure 7.3.
Participation in higher education of students whose parents have low levels of education (2009)

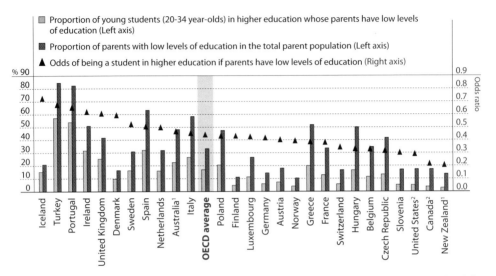

Note: The number of students attending higher education are under-reported for Australia, Canada, New Zealand and the United States compared to the other countries as they only include students who attained ISCED 5A, while the other countries include students who attained ISCED 5A and/or 5B. Therefore, the omission of data on 5B qualifications may understate intergenerational mobility in these countries.
1. Data source from Adult Literacy and Lifeskills Survey (ALL) of 2006.
2. Data source from Adult Literacy and Lifeskills Survey (ALL) of 2003.
Countries are ranked in descending order of the odds of attending higher education.
Source: OECD (2012), *Education at a Glance 2012: OECD Indicators*, OECD Publishing. Table A6.1. See Annex 3 for notes (*www.oecd.org/edu/eag2012*).

StatLink 🖳📥 http://dx.doi.org/10.1787/888932661934

Top performers in science generally attend schools with relatively privileged students and often private, though in some systems the link to social background is weaker: Top performers in science at age 15 tend to be in schools where others are also high performers and from relatively advantaged socio-economic backgrounds. Many such schools select students according to their academic record and many of them are private. Typically, about a quarter of top performers in science come from a socio-economic background below the country's average but in Japan, Finland and Austria, and the partner economies Macao-China and Hong Kong-China, a third or more of the top performers in science come from such a lower socio-economic background. Male students are slightly more likely than females to be top performers in science (1.0% of girls and 1.5% of boys).

📖 *Top of the Class: High Performers in Science in PISA 2006*, 2009, Chapter 2; *PISA 2009 Results: What Students Know and Can Do: Student Performance in Reading, Mathematics and Science*, 2010, Chapter 3

Socially advantaged and female students spend more time in regular lessons and individual study in science, mathematics and the language of instruction: In most countries, socio-economically advantaged students spend much more time in regular school lessons and individual study in science, mathematics and the language of instruction than disadvantaged students: about 11.5 hours per week studying those 3 subjects in regular school lessons compared with 9.8 hours per week for disadvantaged students. This overall OECD difference of 1 hour and 42 minutes per week breaks down into around 50 minutes more per week in science, 30 minutes more mathematics and 20 minutes in the language of instruction. In most countries, females spend around 40 minutes more time in regular school lessons and individual study in science, mathematics and the language of instruction than males.

📖 *Quality Time for Students: Learning In and Out of School,* 2011, Chapter 3

Taking more science courses benefits disadvantaged students even more than it does their more advantaged peers: In general, more time spent learning science results in better performance for the most disadvantaged students. An extra hour of regular science classes increases the likelihood of being resilient (i.e. they do much better in school than might be predicted based on their family circumstances) in all OECD countries except Denmark, Iceland, Portugal, and Mexico. Across OECD countries, on average, the odds of being resilient for disadvantaged students who spend an extra hour a week learning science at school are 1.27 times greater than the odds of disadvantaged students who do not have that opportunity to learn science at school. Exposing disadvantaged students to science learning at school might thus help close performance gaps.

📖 *Against the Odds: Disadvantaged Students who Succeed in School,* 2011, Chapter 3 and Executive Summary

In many OECD countries, tertiary education remains dominated by students from well-educated backgrounds: Evidence from the 1990s showed that young people whose parents had tertiary education themselves were between two and six times as likely to complete tertiary studies as those whose parents had only secondary level qualifications. In 2010, these disparities still existed. On average across OECD countries, a young person from a family with low levels of education is less than one-half (odds of 0.44%) as likely to be in higher education, compared with the proportion of such families in the population. This compares with a young person who has at least one parent with a tertiary degree is almost twice as likely (odds of 1.9) to be in higher education. Only in Denmark, Estonia, Finland, Iceland, Luxembourg, Norway and Sweden is this over-representation of students from high educational backgrounds below 50% (odds below 1.5).

📖 *No More Failures: Ten Steps to Equity in Education,* 2007; *Education at a Glance 2012: OECD Indicators,* 2012, Indicator A6

Engagement in adult learning is far higher among those already well qualified compared with those with low attainment, as it is for younger compared with older adults: On average across OECD countries, someone with tertiary education is almost three times as likely to

be involved in some form of formal or non-formal adult learning programme as those with only low attainment levels. It is even more than 20 percentage points higher than those with the upper secondary level attainment. In countries where adult learning is widespread these gaps tend to be less marked. Twenty-five to thirty-four year-olds with a tertiary education are 2.2 times more likely to participate in formal and/or non-formal education than those with low levels of education. In the 55-64 year-old cohort, highly-educated people are 3.3 times more likely to participate in formal and/or non-formal education than less-educated people. This increased gap associated with different educational attainment levels among the oldest adult group is found in all OECD countries.

📖 *Education at a Glance 2012: OECD Indicators*, 2012, Indicator C6

Recognition of non-formal and informal learning outcomes addresses equity by offering additional opportunities and routes for those who otherwise miss out: First, it can make it easier for dropouts to return to formal learning, giving them a second chance. Second, it can be attractive to groups such as indigenous people and migrants whose competences may otherwise be less recognised, or who have not been able to acquire qualifications through the formal education system. Third, it can help to rebalance equity between generations since a much smaller cohort of older workers had access to higher education and its qualifications than is the case today.

📖 *Recognising Non-formal and Informal Learning: Outcomes, Policies and Practices*, 2010, Executive Summary

Successful school systems provide all students, regardless of their socio-economic backgrounds, with similar opportunities to learn: PISA 2009 analysis shows that successful school systems – those that perform above average and show below-average socio-economic inequalities – provide all students, regardless of their socio-economic backgrounds, with similar opportunities to learn. Systems that show high performance and an equitable distribution of learning outcomes tend to be comprehensive, requiring teachers and schools to embrace diverse student populations through personalised educational pathways. In contrast, school systems that assume that students have different destinations with different expectations and opportunities in terms of how they are placed in schools, classes and grades tend to show less equitable outcomes without an overall performance advantage.

📖 *PISA Results: What Makes a School Successful?: Resources, Policies and Practice*, 2010, Executive summary

POLICY DIRECTIONS

A recent OECD study has followed up the *No More Failures* report to rearticulate five recommendations that can contribute to prevent failure and promote completion of upper secondary education:

- **Eliminate grade repetition:** Grade repetition is costly and ineffective in raising educational outcomes. Alternative strategies include: preventing repetition by addressing learning gaps during the school year; automatic promotion or limiting repetition to subjects or modules failed when there is targeted support; and raising awareness to change public support for repetition.

- **Avoid early tracking and defer student selection to the upper secondary level:** Early student selection has a negative impact on students assigned to lower tracks and exacerbates inequities, without raising average performance. Early student selection should be deferred to upper secondary education. Where there is reluctance to delay early tracking, suppressing lower-level tracks is an alternative.

- **Manage school choice to avoid segregation and increased inequities:** Providing full parental school choice can result in segregating students by ability and socio-economic background, and generate greater inequities across systems. Policies should be designed and managed to balance choice availability against negative equity consequences. Incentives to make disadvantaged students attractive to high-quality schools, influencing school selection mechanisms, and vouchers or tax credits represent different options. Policies are also required to improve disadvantaged families' access to information about schools and to support informed choices.

- **Make funding strategies responsive to students' and schools' needs:** To promote equity and quality across systems, funding strategies should: guarantee access to quality early childhood education and care, especially for disadvantaged families; use funding strategies, such as weighted funding formulae, that factor in possible higher instructional costs. Local autonomy needs to be balanced with resource accountability so as not to undermine support for the most disadvantaged students and schools.

- **Design equivalent upper secondary education pathways to ensure completion:** Upper secondary education is a strategic level of education for individuals and societies; between 10 and 30% of the young people starting do not complete it. Improving the quality and design of upper secondary education can make it more relevant for students and improve completion. There are different policy options: making academic and vocational tracks equivalent by improving the quality of the vocational tracks; facilitating transitions from academic to vocational studies and removing dead ends; reinforcing guidance and counselling for students; and designing targeted measures to prevent dropout – such as additional pathways to obtain an upper secondary qualification or providing incentives to stay in school until completion.

📖 *Equity and Quality in Education: Supporting Disadvantaged Students and Schools,* 2012, Chapter 2; *No More Failures: Ten Steps to Equity in Education,* 2007

The *Equity and Quality in Education* study identified five further policy recommendations addressing low performing disadvantaged schools:

- **Strengthen and support school leadership:** School leadership is the starting point for the transformation of low performing disadvantaged schools but often, school leaders are not well selected, prepared or supported to exercise this transformation role. Leadership preparation programmes should provide both general expertise and specialised knowledge to handle the challenges of these schools. Coaching, mentoring and networks can further support leaders. To attract and retain competent leaders, policies need to

provide good working conditions, systemic support and incentives, with support for restructuring when necessary.

- **Stimulate a supportive school climate and environment for learning:** Low-performing disadvantaged schools risk being poor environments for learning. Policies for them need to focus especially on prioritising positive teacher-student and peer relationships; promoting data information systems for schools to identify struggling students and factors related to learning disruptions; adequate student counseling and mentoring to support students to continue in education. These schools may benefit from an alternative organisation of learning time or size of groups or institutions: the duration of the school week or year or creating smaller classrooms and schools to reinforce interactions and learning strategies.

- **Attract, support and retain high-quality teachers:** Disadvantaged schools are too often not staffed with the highest quality teachers. Policies must raise teacher quality for disadvantaged schools and students by: providing targeted teacher education to develop the skills and knowledge for working in schools with disadvantaged students; providing mentoring programmes for novice teachers; developing supportive working conditions to improve teacher effectiveness and increase teacher retention; and develop adequate financial and career incentives to attract and retain high-quality teachers in disadvantaged schools.

- **Ensure effective classroom learning strategies:** To improve learning in classrooms, policies need to ensure that disadvantaged schools promote the use of a balanced combination of student-centred instruction with aligned curricular and assessment practices. Schools and teachers should use diagnostic tools and formative and summative assessments to monitor children's progress and their knowledge and understanding. Schools should follow a curriculum promoting a culture of high expectations and success.

- **Prioritise the connections between schools and parents and communities:** Disadvantaged parents tend to be less involved in their children's schooling. The schools should prioritise their links with parents and communities, including communication strategies to align school and parental efforts. The more effective strategies target parents who are difficult to reach and encourage individuals from the same communities to mentor students. Building links with the communities around schools, both business and social stakeholders, can also strengthen schools and their students.

📖 *Equity and Quality in Education: Supporting Disadvantaged Students and Schools,* 2012, Chapter 3

Many of the factors involved in improving teaching and teacher education for cultural diversity are identical with good practice in general; others are specific to the challenges of diversity:

- **Develop a shared vision on the nature of increasingly diverse populations**, at different levels and with a variety of stakeholders on how these are reflected in schools and classrooms, and how to accommodate changing landscapes.

- **Improve the diversity of student teachers and teachers**, calling for holistic policy plans within countries and regions for attracting, retaining and inserting diverse student teachers into the teaching force.

- **Promote awareness of contextual specificity and preparation for teaching diverse student populations in pre-service and in-service teacher programmes**, from general principles of working in diverse educational contexts to teaching specific student populations.

- **Focus on improving the attraction and retention of diverse student teachers and teachers**, who can serve as important role models and bring different perspectives into the classroom.

- **Focus on attracting and retaining well-qualified teachers in diverse schools**, understanding better how to do it and implementing necessary measures.

- **Encourage timely, relevant and coherent data collection about who is in the diverse classroom landscape** for more informed decision-making on how best to respond.

📖 *Educating Teachers for Diversity: Meeting the Challenge,* 2010, Chapter 13

OECD analysis on the performance of immigrant students has identified policy orientations to address their less favourable outcomes. These include:

- **Learning the host language needs to be reinforced, both for very young immigrant children and for those students who arrive later with little knowledge of the host country language:** There should not be reliance on the "natural" language-learning ability of young children or on the assumption that a basic level of language proficiency will suffice.. The language skills of parents, particularly of mothers, may not be sufficient to allow them to assist their children in their schoolwork. There needs to be intensive exposure to the host country language, both in and out of school, especially as, in the Internet age, media in the language of the country of origin is more accessible in immigrant households than it ever used to be. Parents need to be sensitised so that the home environment contributes to improving outcomes.

- **Address the concentration of disadvantage:** One relatively costly option is to invest heavily in disadvantaged schools on the expectation that educational measures, whether in the form of better teachers, smaller classes or more remedial help, can improve outcomes, even under unfavourable conditions. A different policy choice involves attempting to reduce the degree of concentration through housing or school choice policies, options that are difficult to implement and controversial. A more balanced social mix in schools would make a significant contribution to improving outcomes for both immigrant and non-immigrant students from disadvantaged backgrounds. All of these policies need to be implemented sufficiently early before immigrant children fall too far behind.

📖 *Untapped Skills: Realising the Potential of Immigrant Students,* 2012, Executive Summary; *Languages in a Global World: Learning for Better Cultural Understanding,* 2012

Actively engaging immigrant parents and communities in education represents an important goal in improving equity: Parental and community involvement involving immigrant groups and families represent key directions for building positive attitudes and conditions for achievement, as well as enriching school systems. Among the promising directions being followed in different countries and localities are:

- Providing adequate information through various communication channels.
- Establishing partnerships between schools and parents.
- Building national platforms for immigrant parents.
- Involving parents in early childhood education and care.
- Involving parents in classroom instruction.
- Assisting and up-skilling immigrant parents.
- Setting up "ethnic mentoring /role model" programmes.
- Encouraging community involvement in providing opportunities for young immigrants.
- Providing additional learning time and after-school support.

📖 *Closing the Gap for Immigrant Students: Policies, Practice and Performance,* 2010, Chapter 3

PISA 2009 analysis of equity in learning opportunities and outcomes suggested certain policy options, to be considered in combination:

- **Targeting low performance regardless of background, either by targeting low-performing schools or low-performing students within schools,** depending on the concentration of such low performance by school.
- **Targeting disadvantaged children through specialised curricula, additional instructional resources or economic assistance for these students.** Policies can address either the school or individual level, depending on the strength of the inter-school social gradient and the extent to which schools are segregated by socio-economic background.
- **Policies targeted at the performance of disadvantaged children can also be used to provide additional economic resources to these students,** for example, free transportation and free lunch programmes or transfer payments for students from poor families.
- **More universal policies aimed at raising standards for all students,** for example, by altering the content and pace of the curriculum or increasing time in language classes. These types of policies are likely to be most relevant in countries with flatter gradients and less variation in student performance.
- **Policies that strive to include marginalised students into mainstream schools and classrooms,** concentrating on including students with disabilities in regular classrooms rather than segregating them in special classes or schools.

📖 *PISA Results 2009: Overcoming Social Background: Equity in Learning Opportunities and Outcomes,* 2010, Policy Implications

References and Further Reading

Della Chiesa, B., J. Scott and **C. Hinton (eds.)** (2012), *Languages in a Global World: Learning for Better Cultural Understanding*, Educational Research and Innovation, OECD Publishing.

Field, S., M. Kuczera and **B. Pont** (2007), *No More Failures: Ten Steps to Equity in Education, Education and Training Policy*, OECD Publishing.

OECD (2006), *Where Immigrant Students Succeed: A Comparative Review of Performance and Engagement in PISA 2003*, OECD Publishing.

OECD (2006), *Demand-sensitive Schooling? Evidence and Issues*, OECD Publishing.

OECD (2008), *Students with Disabilities, Learning Difficulties and Disadvantages: Policies, Statistics and Indicators – 2007 Edition*, OECD Publishing.

OECD (2009), *Top of the Class: High Performers in Science in PISA 2006*, OECD Publishing.

Werquin (2010), *Recognising Non-formal and Informal Learning: Outcomes, Polices and Practices* (by Patrick Werquin), OECD Publishing.

OECD (2010), *Educating Teachers for Diversity: Meeting the Challenge*, OECD Publishing.

OECD (2010), *Education at a Glance 2010: OECD Indicators*, OECD Publishing.

OECD (2010), *Are the New Millennium Learners Making the Grade? Technology Use and Educational Performance in PISA*, OECD Publishing.

OECD (2010), *Closing the Gap for Immigrant Students: Policies, Practice and Performance*, OECD Publishing.

OECD (2010), *PISA Results 2009: What Students Know and Can Do: Student Performance in Reading, Mathematics and Science (Volume I)*, OECD Publishing.

OECD (2010), *PISA Results 2009: Overcoming Social Background: Equity in Learning Opportunities and Outcomes (Volume II)*, OECD Publishing.

OECD (2010), *PISA Results: What Makes a School Successful?: Resources, Policies and Practice (Volume IV)*, OECD Publishing.

OECD (2010), *PISA Results 2009: Learning Trends: Change in Student Performance Since 2000 (Volume V)*, OECD Publishing.

OECD (2011), *Against the Odds: Disadvantaged Students Who Succeed in School*, OECD Publishing.

OECD (2011), *Quality Time for Students: Learning In and Out of School*, OECD Publishing.

OECD (2012), *Equity and Quality in Education: Supporting Disadvantaged Students and Schools*, OECD Publishing.

OECD (2011), *PISA in Focus, Issue No. 2, March 2011*, OECD Publishing.

OECD (2012), *Untapped Skills: Realising the Potential of Immigrant Students*, OECD Publishing.

OECD (2012), *Education at a Glance 2012: OECD Indicators*, OECD Publishing.

8

Innovation and Knowledge Management

Recognition of the key role of research and knowledge management in educational practice and policy making is in general recent. The volume of relevant educational research and development (R&D) tends to be low, despite education being so explicitly about knowledge, and there has been only weak capacity to develop and exploit the knowledge base on which to build improved practice and effective policies. A great deal of educational change is still shaped by short-term considerations despite education's fundamental long-term mission and nature. Improving the knowledge base and fostering innovation have been the aims of policy in a number of countries. Within the OECD, analyses of educational R&D systems, knowledge management, innovative practice including using technology, systemic innovation, futures thinking, and evidence-informed policy and practice, have all been prominent. Analysis has also focused on the so-called 21st century skills, seen as fundamental to innovative and creative societies.

INTRODUCTION

Innovation is a longstanding focus of educational work at the OECD - the Centre for Educational Research and Innovation (CERI) was founded over 40 years ago. This Centre has provided the educational contribution to the OECD-wide "Innovation Strategy", which focus continues. Recently-completed work on "New Millennium Learners" looked especially at how education systems can best use and develop the skills for technology, including through technology-rich innovation. *PISA 2009 Results: Students Online* complements this by providing a comparative insight into the digital competence of students. The "Innovative Learning Environments" project has compiled and analysed examples of innovations that reconfigure the way that learning takes place and in future will investigate effective strategies for scaling and sustaining 21st century learning environments.

Recognition of the key role of research and knowledge management in educational practice and policy making has been growing but still tends to be weakly developed. In many countries, there has been only limited capacity to develop and exploit the knowledge base on which improved practice and effective policies can be based. The volume of relevant educational research and development (R&D) tends generally to be low, despite education being so explicitly about knowledge. Similarly, a great deal of educational change is still shaped by short-term considerations despite education's fundamental long-term mission and nature. Educational R&D systems, knowledge management, futures thinking, and evidence-informed policy and practice, have all been prominent aspects of the research and innovation work of the OECD in education.

KEY FINDINGS

For a person, organisation, economy or society to be innovative requires wide-ranging skills, including "soft skills", raising questions about how effectively education systems foster them: Innovation covers a wide range of activities, from invention and breakthroughs, to implementation and minor improvements. It therefore necessitates a wide variety of skills:

- **Basic skills and digital age literacy:** Reading, writing and numeracy, and the skills to use digital technology, and to access and interpret information.

- **Academic skills:** Languages, mathematics, history, law and science, these skills are generally obtained through the education system and are transferable across different situations.

- **Technical skills:** The specific skills needed in an occupation, maybe both academic and vocational, as well as knowledge of certain tools or processes.

- **Generic skills:** Skills of this sort commonly are seen to include problem-solving, critical and creative thinking, ability to learn, and ability to manage complexity. A skill such as problem-solving may be considered as transferable, but some argue that it is also firm-specific.

- **"Soft" skills:** Working in teams and heterogeneous groups, communication, motivation, volition and initiative, the ability to read and manage one's own and others' emotions and behaviours, multicultural openness, and receptiveness to innovation.

- **Leadership:** Related to "soft" skills, these include team-building and steering, coaching and mentoring, lobbying and negotiating, co-ordination, ethics and charisma.

📖 *The OECD Innovation Strategy: Getting a Head Start on Tomorrow,* 2010, Chapter 3

Schools are conventionally poor at using the key motors of innovation – research knowledge, networking, modular restructuring, technological advance: OECD work on knowledge management has identified four key "pumps of innovation":

- **The "science-based" innovation pump**: Education has not traditionally made enough direct use of research knowledge, and there is often cultural resistance to doing so. This is increasingly being targeted in reform.

- **The "horizontally-organised" innovation pump:** There are obvious benefits in terms of teachers pooling their knowledge through networks, but incentives to do so remain underdeveloped. There is need to tighten the "loose coupling" between the single teachers, individual classrooms and individual schools that so characterise school systems.

- **The "modular structures" pump:** This is about building complex processes from smaller sub-systems that are designed independently, but function together. Education is accustomed to working in modules, but much of it involves schools or teachers operating separately from each other.

- **The "information and communication technologies" (ICT) pump:** There is a powerful potential for ICT to transform education, but its use in schools remains underdeveloped, partly because the main *modus operandi* of school administration and instruction are resistant to change.

📖 *Innovation in the Knowledge Economy: Implications for Education and Learning,* 2004, Chapter 2

The growing focus on educational outcomes has resulted in both an explosion of evidence of different kinds and a policy thirst for the results of educational research: There is a mounting preoccupation with what happens as a result of educational investments and participation, rather than the primary focus being on these inputs. Outcomes cover not only course completion and qualifications, but also skills and competences (as with the PISA surveys), access to and success in the labour market, and wider social outcomes, such as health and citizenship, attributable to education. There has been a huge expansion of evidence resulting from the growing volume of testing and assessment activities. As policy increasingly focuses on what education actually delivers, so is there interest in the information coming from research, but we know too little about how this evidence is used and whether it is used effectively.

📖 *Evidence in Education: Linking Research and Policy,* 2007, Chapter 1

For most OECD countries, it has become clear that *promoting* the use of evidence in policy making is not the same thing as *ensuring* its use: The limited time and capacity of policy makers, the need to build on consensus and incorporate public opinion, and the interaction among different forms of knowledge when determining the best course of action are all limitations to the effective uptake of research. In addition, the analytical capacity of organisations to use complex and multiple sources of information is influenced by institutional culture and the importance given to using research (including the role of media). Governments committed to using research evidence in policy-making must address the individual and organisational barriers to doing so.

📖 "Exploring the Complex Interaction Between Governance and Knowledge in Education", *OECD Education Working Papers*, No. 67, 2012

On average OECD countries spend close to a third of their annual expenditure per tertiary student on R&D: In 2009, expenditure on R&D represents on average 31% of total expenditure per tertiary student across OECD countries. These levels vary widely: from 40% or more of total expenditure per tertiary student in Norway, Portugal, Sweden and Switzerland to less than 15% in Chile, Korea, the Slovak Republic and the United States. Even where R&D is less than 40% of expenditure at the tertiary level, this represents a considerable amount. For example in the United Kingdom, 39.5% of expenditure amounts to more than USD 6 400 per student. The OECD countries with highest R&D activity in tertiary educational institutions (e.g. Portugal, Sweden and Switzerland) tend to report higher expenditure per student than those in which a large proportion of R&D takes place in other public institutions or in industry (e.g. the United States).

📖 *Education at a Glance 2012: OECD Indicators,* 2012, Indicator B1

Figure 8.1.
Annual expenditure on R&D per tertiary student in OECD countries (2009)

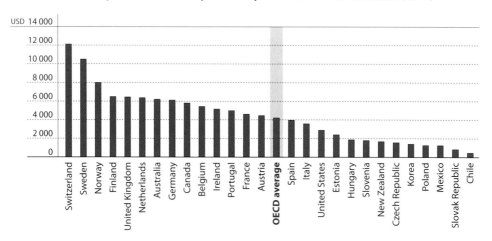

Source: OECD (2012), *Education at a Glance 2012: OECD Indicators,* OECD Publishing. Table B1.2. See Annex 3 for notes (www.oecd.org/edu/eag2012).

StatLink ᴍᴤ⬛ http://dx.doi.org/10.1787/xxxxxxxxxxxx

Box 8.1. **Innovative educational technologies**

Information and communication technology (ICT) is a source of innovation in education systems: ICT offers potentially a wide range of new tools and instruments to change the technological, organisational and institutional foundations of the education sector. Education has tended to be slow to generate and exploit innovations to improve practices but an educational tool industry is now emerging: the spread of small firms specialised in inventing and commercialising (mainly ICT-based) instruction technologies.

Number of top 50 companies with a specialised education patent portfolio in specific markets (2010)

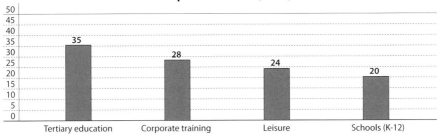

Source: Foray, D. and J. Raffo (2012), "Business-Driven Innovation: Is It Making a Difference in Education?: An Analysis of Patents", *OECD Education Working Papers*, No. 84, OECD Publishing.

Analysis of education-related patents over the past 20 years shows a clear rise in the production of highly innovative educational technologies by businesses, typically building on advances in information and communication technology.

Yet, the emerging educational tool industry currently targets other markets than the formal primary and secondary education sector. An in-depth analysis of the top 50 specialised companies in patenting educational tools revealed that 35 out of the top 50 specialised firms operate in the tertiary education market, while only 20 operate in the schooling sector. Fewer companies commercialise their inventions in the formal primary and secondary education system than in the other market segments. This market does probably not satisfy most conditions for attracting and sustaining strong entrepreneurial activity. Could the public school system better exploit the opportunities offered by the development of a tool industry? Is there enough innovation friendliness in the public sector in terms of management practices, governance and culture, as well as funding and resource allocation logics? These are some of the issues for education decision-makers to address.

📖 Foray, D. and J. Raffo (2012), "Business-Driven Innovation: Is It Making a Difference in Education?: An Analysis of Patents", *OECD Education Working Papers*, No. 84, OECD Publishing.

Over the past decade, many countries have implemented one-to-one computing initiatives in education to provide young people with ICT skills, reduce the digital divide, and enhance educational practice and achievement. OECD analysis shows that:

- Despite the large sums of money invested, **there is little evidence about the cost-effectiveness of these initiatives.** Every one-to-one programme should be evaluated from the beginning of the process in ways that are coherent with the goals and design of the initiative.

- The presence of ICT devices **does not necessarily change teaching and learning strategies,** and the use of ICT devices in 1:1 initiatives varies widely. Teachers need clear goals and specific support to incorporate learning technologies into innovative pedagogical practices.

- **Evaluations point to a positive impact of 1:1 computing on ICT skills and writing,** but more modest positive evidence regarding other academic domains such as mathematics.

- **Large-scale 1:1 initiatives could limit the first digital divide in the access to ICT at home and in school.** The globalisation of 1:1 initiatives could help reduce the digital divide between developed and developing countries.

- **A second digital divide emerges in school when all the learners have access to ICT devices.** More evidence is necessary about how ICT are used in class and its impact on achievement.

📖 "1-1 in Education", *OECD Education Working Papers,* No. 44, 2010

There is widespread development and activity in open educational resources (OER): OECD countries are mostly active with OER by involvement with specific projects or programmes or through the initiative of institutions or engaged individuals. The most frequently-cited policy reason for OER activity is the desire to increase access to high-quality learning materials. Several countries, especially those with federal systems, indicate that they have insufficient knowledge about the OER activities in their educational institutions. In contrast to the understanding that situates OER mainly on the post-secondary educational level, OER activity was spread more widely across the educational spectrum.

📖 "Open Educational Resources: Analysis of Responses to the OECD Questionnaire", *OECD Education Working Papers,* No. 76, 2012

OECD work on *New Millennium Learners* has provided insights into how best use and develop the skills for technology, including through technology-rich innovation:

- **The knowledge economy and society are permeated and supported by connectedness and technology:** This has important implications for education, firstly, because education has to equip younger generations with the range of skills that are demanded by a knowledge economy, and second, connectedness plays a crucial role in new forms of socialisation and identity formation.

- **In OECD countries, a large majority of young people, starting at an increasingly early age, already benefit from connectedness:** Younger people have a greater range of digital technologies at home, have higher levels of Internet self efficacy, multi-task more, and use the Internet for fact-checking and formal learning activities.

- **Being more connected is not always a good thing;** what matters is what young people do while they are connected.

- **Young people's expectations and behaviours in relation to technology use or connectivity in education are not changing dramatically:** Learners are not always comfortable with innovative uses of technology in formal education despite their social practices outside of education. They **do** expect technology to be a source of engagement, to make school or academic work more convenient, and to make them much more educationally productive.

📖 *Connected Minds: Technology and Today's Learners,* 2012, Chapter 8

POLICY DIRECTIONS

The OECD's horizontal "Innovation Strategy", in considering how people can be empowered to innovate, concluded with a set of "policy principles" about education and training systems, and innovative workplaces. These tend to parallel closely more general conclusions about education and training policy:

- **Equip people with skills for innovation:** Ensure that education and training systems are adaptable, and can accommodate the changing nature of innovation and the demands of the future. Curricula and pedagogies should develop the capacity to learn new skills and take full advantage of information and communications technologies.

- **Improve educational outcomes:** A considerable share of children still do not complete upper secondary education or leave schools with poor literacy and numeracy skills. While virtually all young people in OECD countries have access to at least 12 years of formal education, mechanisms are needed to ensure that solid educational foundations are universal.

- **Continue to reform tertiary education systems:** Public authorities should enable tertiary education institutions to become catalysts for innovation, notably in their local and regional settings. While the steering role should be reserved for government, institutions should have considerable room for manoeuvre. The tertiary sector also needs to retain sufficient diversity to respond to future needs in the innovation system.

- **Connect vocational education and training to the world of work:** This requires a good balance between occupationally-specific skills that meet employers' needs and generic transferable skills that equip graduates for lifelong learning and mobility.

- **Enable women to play a larger role in the innovation process:** Although female educational attainment tends now to outstrip that of men, the tax and benefit systems, and workplace practices and childcare are key to fuller engagement by women in the labour force and innovation.

- **Support international mobility:** Policies should support knowledge flows and the creation of enduring linkages across countries. Migration regimes for the highly skilled should be efficient, transparent and simple; enable short-term movements; and support connections to nationals abroad.

- **Foster innovative workplaces:** Employee involvement and effective labour management help to foster creativity and innovation, and employment policies should encourage efficient organisational change. Learning and interaction within firms are key to their innovation performance; governments may also shape national institutions to support higher levels of employee learning and training.

 📖 *The OECD Innovation Strategy: Getting a Head Start on Tomorrow,* 2010, Chapter 3

Effective decision-making means to be informed as far as possible by evidence, with educational professionals working in a "knowledge-rich" environment: There is need for better links between educational research, policy and practice, and for further progress towards making education a knowledge-rich profession. Greater access to web-based information goes hand-in-hand with less quality control, alongside a shift in most OECD countries towards more decentralised decision-making in education. Given greater information, less quality control, a more informed public and a greater diversity of policy-makers, the need for clear, reliable and easily available evidence on which to base decisions has become more important than ever before, as has the need to find mechanisms to obtain reliable answers to pressing policy questions.

 📖 *Evidence in Education: Linking Research and Policy,* 2007, Chapter 1

Create and encourage knowledge brokerage in education systems: Brokerage agencies are increasingly important to encourage dialogue between policy-makers, researchers and educators, and to build capacity to evaluate what does and does not work. An important first step is to create a database of quality research on key topics of interest to policy makers, and to provide clear goals for conducting and evaluating educational research. A key component of these brokerage agencies is the transparent exchange of findings with their methodologies clearly defined, with commitment to update and maintain state-of-the-art syntheses on core topics. And, all centres should seek to disseminate to as wide an audience as possible in order to effect both top-down and bottom-up change.

 📖 *Evidence in Education: Linking Research and Policy,* 2007, Chapter 1

Governments can foster investments and stimulate the production of digital learning resources (DLRs) both by commercial companies/publishers and users by:

- **Offering seed money, supplemented with development and transition funds:** The production of DLRs can be stimulated by offering public tender seed money to publishers, supplemented by development project funding and support to help keep innovations afloat once the initial project funding has ended.

- **Promoting co-operation between public and private players for DLR development:** Governments can encourage companies to develop corporate social responsibility programmes and to increase co-operation with public authorities in education. Schools and local educational authorities will need guidelines on how best to approach such co-operation.

📖 *Beyond Textbooks: Digital Learning Resources as Systemic Innovation in the Nordic Countries,* 2009, Chapter 7

A systemic approach to innovation in VET is urgent: Precisely in times of economic crisis, innovation is increasingly a key factor, not only for economic growth, but also for social welfare. A recent study of systemic innovation in the VET sector suggested the following guiding policy principles:

- Develop a systemic approach to innovation in VET as a guiding principle for innovation-related policies.
- Promote a continuous and evidence-informed dialogue about innovation with the VET stakeholders.
- Build a well-organised, formalised, easy to access, and updated knowledge base about VET as a prerequisite for successfully internalising the benefits of innovation.
- Supplement investments in VET innovations with the necessary efforts in monitoring and evaluation.
- Support relevant research on VET according to national priorities and link these efforts to innovation.

📖 *Working Out Change: Systemic Innovation in Vocational Education and Training,* 2009, Chapter 10

Create an effective interface between innovation and higher education systems: Such an interface is needed in order to reap the benefits from public and private investments in research, and to ensure the vitality and quality of higher education systems. Directions for creating such an interface include:

- **Improve knowledge diffusion rather than commercialisation via stronger intellectual property rights (IPRs):** Innovation is not only a discovery process to then be commercialised but R&D is often problem-solving along a pathway of innovation. The diffusion capabilities and support activities of tertiary education institutions may thus be as important as discovery processes, and should be promoted by policy.

- **Improve and widen channels of interaction, and encourage inter-institutional collaboration:** Linkages between the tertiary education sector and other actors in the research and innovation system, such as firms and public research organisations, need to be actively developed to ensure effective knowledge diffusion. When programmes are designed, they need to consider the engagement of small- and medium-sized enterprises from all technological sectors as they tend to be under-represented in such collaborations.

- **Foster mobility across the research and innovation system**: Inter-sectoral mobility is one of the main vehicles for knowledge diffusion; mobility between firms, tertiary education institutions and public research organisation should be actively promoted.

📖 *Tertiary Education for the Knowledge Society: Volume 2,* 2008, Chapter 7

OECD work on ICT and education has provided policy pointers for educational systems looking to scale up technology-based innovations to improve learning, especially regarding knowledge needs:

- **Develop a systemic approach to knowledge about technology innovation,** with an evolving framework for sustaining both top-down and bottom-up technology-based innovations and appropriate capacity building.

- **Promote a continuous and evidence-informed dialogue about innovation with stakeholders in the field:** policy debate needs to be informed by evidence, presupposing that all stakeholders share a minimum capacity to engage in it.

- **Build a well-organised, easily accessible, and up-to-date knowledge base about technology in education, as a prerequisite for successfully internalising the benefits of innovation:** existing facilities or mechanisms may be used or else set up new measures to reflect the increased priority for technology-based innovation in education, such as dedicated research centres, networks or prioritised calls.

- **Supplement investments in technology-based innovations with the necessary monitoring and evaluation:** Public governance and accountability require mechanisms and procedures to critically approach both bottom-up and top-down innovations. Empirical assessments can contribute to informing decisions about scaling or diffusing innovations, instilling a culture of output-oriented innovation, getting value for money, and obtaining feedback on policy measures intended to foster innovation.

- **Support relevant research on technology in education according to national priorities and link these efforts to innovation:** Education systems would greatly benefit from a national system of educational research on technology.

- **Ensure that technology-based innovations do not reinforce existing digital divides or create new ones:** Computer use amplifies a student's academic skills and competences, and these competences are related to the student's social, cultural and economic capital. This becomes the more serious as access to computers and broadband internet connection has become quasi-universal.

- **Align or embed strategies for technology-based innovations with national policies for educational quality and equity:** Having a separate technology strategy for education can be valuable to signal its importance but to be sustainable it will need to be well aligned with national policies for quality and equity in education and become a means to the end of good learning rather than an end in itself.

📖 *Inspired by Technology, Driven by Pedagogy: A Systematic Approach to Technology-Based School Innovations,* 2010, Conclusion

References and Further Reading

Fazekas, M. and **T. Burns** (2012), "Exploring the Complex Interaction Between Governance and Knowledge in Education", *OECD Education Working Papers*, No. 67, OECD Publishing.

Foray, D. and **J. Raffo** (2012) "Business-Driven Innovation: Is It Making a Differebnce in Education?: An Analaysis of Patents", *OECD Education Working Papers,* No. 84, OECD Publishing.

Hylén, J. et al. (2012), "Open Educational Resources: Analysis of Responses to the OECD Country Questionnaire", *OECD Education Working Papers*, No. 76, OECD Publishing.

OECD (2004), *Innovation in the Knowledge Economy: Implications for Education and Learning*, OECD Publishing.

OECD (2007), *Evidence in Education: Linking Research and Policy,* OECD Publishing.

OECD (2008), *Tertiary Education for the Knowledge Society: Volume 2*, OECD Publishing.

OECD (2009), *Working Out Change: Systemic Innovation in Vocational Education and Training*, OECD Publishing.

OECD (2009), *Beyond Textbooks: Digital Learning Resources as Systemic Innovation in the Nordic Countries*, OECD Publishing.

OECD (2010), *The OECD Innovation Strategy: Getting a Head Start on Tomorrow*, OECD Publishing.

OECD (2010), *Inspired by Technology, Driven by Pedagogy: A Systematic Approach to Technology-Based School Innovations,* OECD Publishing.

OECD (2011), *PISA 2009 Results: Students On Line: Digital Technologies and Performance (Volume VI),* OECD Publishing.

OECD (2012), *Connected Minds: Technology and Today's Learners.* OECD Publishing.

OECD (2012), *Education at a Glance 2012: OECD Indicators,* OECD Publishing.

Valiente, O. (2010), "1-1 in Education: Current Practice, International Comparative Research Evidence and Policy Implications", *OECD Education Working Papers*, No. 44, OECD Publishing.

More information on OECD's work on education

Write to us

Directorate for Education
OECD
2, rue André Pascal, 75775 Paris Cedex 16, France
edu.contact@oecd.org

Connect with us on

 Educationtoday: Global perspectives on Education:
http://oecdeducationtoday.blogspot.fr/

 YouTube: *www.youtube.com/EDUcontact*

Twitter: *http://twitter.com/OECD_Edu*

 Slideshare: *www.slideshare.net/OECDEDU*

How to apply for a job

Current job vacancies are open to nationals of OECD member countries
and are published on *www.oecd.org/hrm*

In addition, the OECD Directorate for Education works with a network
of external consultatnts, universities and research intitutes. Calls for tender
for the projects in the area of education are published on *www.oecd.org/pcm*

Order our publications

OECD iLibrary through the OECD on-line bookshop: *www.oecd.org/bookshop*
Browse it online before you buy or by sending an e-mail to *sales@oecd.org*

MYBROCHUREOECD Select and download a pdf file of the brochure "OECD Work on Education":
http://oecdmybrochure.org/

Get free education reports and statistics

www.oecd.org/education for a selection of free downloadable OECD reports
and data,

www.oecd.org/edu/workingpapers for a series of education working papers,
and

www.pisa.oecd.org for the Programme for International Student Assessment
(PISA) data.

OECDdirect Be the first to know the latest OECD publications on education with
our free e-mail alert service: *www.oecd.org/login*

ORGANISATION FOR ECONOMIC CO-OPERATION AND DEVELOPMENT

The OECD is a unique forum where governments work together to address the economic, social and environmental challenges of globalisation. The OECD is also at the forefront of efforts to understand and to help governments respond to new developments and concerns, such as corporate governance, the information economy and the challenges of an ageing population. The Organisation provides a setting where governments can compare policy experiences, seek answers to common problems, identify good practice and work to co-ordinate domestic and international policies.

The OECD member countries are: Australia, Austria, Belgium, Canada, Chile, the Czech Republic, Denmark, Estonia, Finland, France, Germany, Greece, Hungary, Iceland, Ireland, Israel, Italy, Japan, Korea, Luxembourg, Mexico, the Netherlands, New Zealand, Norway, Poland, Portugal, the Slovak Republic, Slovenia, Spain, Sweden, Switzerland, Turkey, the United Kingdom and the United States. The European Union takes part in the work of the OECD.

OECD Publishing disseminates widely the results of the Organisation's statistics gathering and research on economic, social and environmental issues, as well as the conventions, guidelines and standards agreed by its members.

OECD PUBLISHING, 2, rue André-Pascal, 75775 PARIS CEDEX 16
(96 2012 02 1P) ISBN 978-92-64-17710-9 – No. 60401 2012-05